SHIRE GARDEN HISTORY

Garden Sculpture

Michael Symes

Triton fountain by Mozani; Waddesdon Manor, Buckinghamshire.

Published in 1996 by Shire Publications Ltd, Cromwell House, Church Street, Princes Risborough, Buckinghamshire HP27 9AA, UK.

Printed in Great Britain by CIT Printing Services, Press Buildings, Merlins Bridge, Haverfordwest, Dyfed SA61 1XF.

British Library Cataloguing in Publication Data: Symes, Michael. Garden Sculpture. - (Shire garden history; no. 8) 1. Garden ornaments and furniture - Great Britain - History. 2. Nymphaea (Architecture) - Great Britain - History. 3. Sculpture, British - History I. Title 730.9'41. ISBN 0-7478-0320-X.

ACKNOWLEDGEMENTS
Photographs are by the author, except for the following: John Anthony, page 24 (bottom); Bulbeck Foundry, page 10 (both); Cadbury Lamb, pages 3, 5 (left), 16 (top), 46 (left), 50, 51, 66 (bottom), 80 (top), 85 (right).

Lion Attacking a Horse by Peter Scheemakers; Rousham, Oxfordshire.

Contents

Bronze group of horse and dragon, Stratfield Saye, Hampshire. Commissioned by George IV from Matthew Cotes Wyatt for St George's Hall, Windsor Castle, it was originally intended to include St George but the King died before it was complete.

Introduction

Sculpture can add life and character to a garden; it can focus attention and direct the eye; it may have a symbolic or iconographical meaning; it can mark key points in an axis or walk, such as on the skyline at the top of an ascent up an allée. It can be serious or playful, have a purpose or be purely ornamental. In some gardens, or areas within a garden, sculpture may be the most important element.

The setting of a piece of sculpture in a garden can be crucial, so that the surrounding garden area shows the piece off to especial advantage. Some particular representations (usually classical) recur in gardens and seem to lend themselves well to outdoor location, yet the same figures may have equal effect inside a building or in a courtyard or street. Garden sculpture cannot, therefore, be divorced from sculpture in general, but it is true to say that it has its own character and characteristics, determined by the material and the weather.

Figure sculpture is often derived from classical mythology and was intended to have a significance that has been largely lost on modern visitors. It requires an imaginative (and knowledgeable) leap back to recover the sensibilities of the educated visitor of, say, two centuries ago. What might strike many people as quaint today would have been accepted as common cultural coin at the time. Other figures may represent bygone monarchs or other public figures and therefore also require knowledge of history. Modern sculpture may speak more directly to a present-day audience.

In considering the sculpture we see in gardens today, we must be aware that statues may have been moved from one spot to another, which is not uncommon since they are usually relatively portable. Whatever the reason for moving a figure, it may be desirable to ascertain its original location. Placing it somewhere else may considerably affect not just the appearance but also the meaning of a garden. Other figures may have been added over the years, and it may be necessary to determine what relates to the original concept.

Various kinds of sculpture have been imported, especially from Italy, whence both classical and Renaissance statues and busts have arrived in Britain in large numbers over the last few hundred years. These figures have moved far from their original setting and may consequently have a very different effect in their new home.

Thus, although this book is concerned with British garden sculpture, continental influences and imported figures have to be considered.

The term 'sculpture' is used to cover representations of people and creatures (generally called statues), abstract forms such as are found in modern sculpture and also, in a few cases, urns or vases where there is modelling of figures. Topiary is not covered. There are few unfamiliar terms, although the word 'statuary', mostly used today to describe statues or a collection of statues, in the eighteenth century was more commonly used to refer to a maker of statues, or sometimes the firm (or sculptor's yard) which produced them.

I acknowledge the help of several friends in producing this book. My particular thanks go to Malcolm Baker and John Davis, who have read parts of the manuscript, and to Susanne Groom, who provided information on Hampton Court. Sir Reresby Sitwell furnished the history of 'Fame' at Renishaw.

Above: *Mercury, attributed to John Van Nost the Elder; Rousham, Oxfordshire.*

Left: *Shepherd-piper, attributed to John Van Nost the Younger; Canons Ashby, Northamptonshire.*

Materials and techniques

All kinds of materials have been used for sculpture, although in the case of garden sculpture the materials have had to be weather-resistant. Whatever it is made of, sculpture falls into two basic categories: those figures which are carved or otherwise fashioned individually and those which involve a process of casting, allowing in some cases copies of the same figure to be produced. Both kinds of sculpture are to be found from classical times onwards.

For single figures, wood and stone have been the most widely used materials. Since the time of the Greeks wood has been used extensively, but in northern latitudes it rots unless very well protected and can be destroyed by woodworm and beetles. We tend, therefore, not to find much wooden sculpture in British gardens.

Much more common is stone. This covers many types – granite, alabaster (now usually called calcite), sandstones and limestone – and includes the various kinds of marble that are familiar through classical and Renaissance sculpture. Marble is generally white, but sometimes it is of other colours or has veins of varying hues within a basic colour, and it is characterised by its sheen when polished. Particularly prized has been the marble from one or two Italian quarries, the most important of which is Carrara, which produces a cream-white stone. It does not weather well if exposed to the sharper elements, as the figures in the Privy Garden at Hampton Court, Middlesex, show. Four of the five original figures have had to be preserved indoors and replaced by copies; the fifth has survived in better condition because it had been kept in a sheltered location.

In Britain the limestone most commonly used for garden ornament has been Portland stone from Dorset. It has an even, greyish-white colour, a fine texture good for carving and lasts reasonably well outdoors, though many eighteenth-century pieces now show the effects of weathering, which destroys detail. It does, however, survive better than many other stones. Bath stone, a limestone recognisable from its yellow-orange colour, is coarser than Portland stone and more suitable for vases and plinths than for carved figure sculpture; it has been used extensively for buildings, especially in the city of Bath and its environs. Bath stone weathers quite well but attracts more lichens than Portland stone. Among other local limestones may be mentioned Ketton stone (from a quarry near Stamford in Lincolnshire), which was used for local statuary as well as for many of the college buildings at Cambridge; it carves well and wears perhaps even better than Portland stone. Close inspection reveals a texture that has been compared to fish roe.

Local sandstones were sometimes used for vases, finials and pedestals but not often for figure work. The occasional sandstone sculpture to be encountered (such as the French figure of a nymph of Diana at St Paul's Walden Bury, Hertfordshire) is more likely to be an import and does not take kindly to the English climate.

A stone statue is generally sculpted from a block and shaped by hammers and chisels. Sometimes, however, statues were carved in sections which were then joined together, a process known as 'piecing'. Classical statues were often painted in colours appropriate to skin, hair and clothes.

Metal statues are cast in moulds. Bronze casting was brought to a high degree of sophistication by the Greeks, and the basic system, with modifications, has been used since. Known as the 'lost wax' (*cire perdue*) process, the method (reduced to simplest terms which do no justice to the complications and the skill involved) was as follows. A model of the figure was first made in clay or plaster and then covered in wax. A mould, mostly of soft clay, was pressed around the wax and then baked hard. The wax melted out through a hole, leaving a thin gap between the core model and the clay mould outside. Molten bronze would be poured into the gap and would harden to form a skin round the core. The outer mould would be removed to leave the bronze sculpture. The core was removed by various methods.

In a refinement of this process, which enabled the model to be used again, the model was coated in two sections with gelatine and then with supporting clay or plaster. When the clay was dry the two sections were separated and the model was removed. The gelatine interior, which replicates the shape of the original, was coated with melted wax to the required thickness, allowed to harden and then the gelatine was removed. Each half of the wax outline was embedded in clay and filled with grog (crushed stoneware) and plaster. Thin metal stays were driven through the outer clay right into the core so that it remained steady. The sections were joined together and the mould was heated to harden the clay and to melt the wax, which was drained off. The metal was then poured into the space left by the wax.

In the case of lead casting, popular from the end of the seventeenth century, replication of figures became an important commercial consideration. A statue was cast in sections in moulds taken from the model in stone, clay or lead. Clay was pressed around the model and for each section (for example, a limb, or part of a limb) a clay mould was made, divided so that it could be removed. An internal clay core was made and the two parts of the mould assembled round it, leaving a gap of 6-7 mm for the molten lead. The section was cast and left to cool. Then the mould was separated, revealing the lead cast, and put aside for use again; the core inside was broken up and removed. The cast sections were then assembled around a wrought-iron frame, called an armature, sometimes strengthened by other materials such as plaster. The sections were soldered together and rubbed down. Details such as buttons would be added separately, and one copy might well vary from another either in small detail or by the addition or replacement of a separately cast unit. Not all details are known, but most lead figures in the eighteenth century are likely to have been made by this method rather than by the lost wax process. Cast-iron statues, when they appeared, were made by the lost wax method. All these methods were hazardous.

It was common practice to paint lead figures to resemble stone, gilt or bronze, or in naturalistic colours echoing the tones of skin, clothes and accessories to create the illusion of reality. The opposite page shows an eighteenth-century figure of Bacchus which has been restored to its original colour scheme. It is unlikely that any statue at the time was left with a lead finish, for the paint also helped to protect the statue. Care was taken to protect it from the elements once it was in place. John Cheere sent out a statue in 1753 with a recommendation that 'once in two years it should be washed very clean and oyled over with Lintseed oyle'.

In 1769 the Coade artificial stone works opened in Lambeth and started a revolution that spelled the end for the lead manufactories. Under Mrs Eleanor Coade the works produced a kiln-fired vitrified ceramic, based on clay, grog, flint, sand and glass, that could be cast in moulds and therefore duplicated, and which was virtually impervious to the weather and did not attract lichens or other discolouring substances. Coade stone figures still retain remarkable sharpness of detail. Although it has often been mistaken for stone, it has a distinctive, uniform, glowing beige colour (colours sometimes vary) and no veining. The secret of its composition was jealously guarded. Sheets of the clay were pressed into the moulds, which were then fired for up to four days at very high temperatures. Constituent parts of a piece were joined with clay inside and joins skilfully concealed with slip (a paste). It was ideal for garden statuary.

Coade stone continued to be made until the 1840s, by which time a number of rival firms were producing artificial stone from similar processes, and some produced figures. From about 1850

Opposite page: *Bacchus, painted lead; private collection.*

Bulbeck Foundry at Burwell, Cambridgeshire. (Above) Hot lead is poured into a mould. (Below) Behind an almost finished planter is suspended a statue awaiting restoration.

the firm of J. M. Blashfield produced a ceramic body, a clay-based terracotta, one of the most popular garden materials of the nineteenth century and also one which has shown its ability to last; colouring varies from a pale yellow to a brownish orange. Austin & Seeley's artificial limestone, produced from about the late 1820s, was composed of cement, stone pieces, tile and sand and produced a very convincing imitation stone of an admired hardness for such objects as bowls and fountains. From the 1850s Doulton sold a range of figures in durable unglazed terracotta, including the Seasons and the Muses, together with elaborate bordered fountains, vases and many other garden ornaments. Porcelain was also used to a lesser extent.

James Pulham (father and son had the same first name) perfected an artificial stone known as Pulhamite, based on cement. It was extensively used for rockwork in gardens but they also produced weather-resistant terracotta ornaments from 1843. The firm continued until 1945, though concentrating in the twentieth century on terracotta, which included figure work.

During the nineteenth century industrial advances led to a number of new materials for garden ornament. Also mass production enabled items to be produced more cheaply. Cast iron was favoured for such items as gates, railings, seats and fountains, while cast-iron statues, particularly animals, could reach as high a standard as bronze casts. The Coalbrookdale Company of Shropshire was one of the leading manufacturers. Zinc was also used for sculpture, and a zinc-based alloy, spelter, was electroplated to give a bronze-like finish.

Casting is still very much used, whether for single pieces or multiple copies. The German/Polish sculptor Igor Mitoraj, whose work was displayed at the Yorkshire Sculpture Park in 1992-3, carved from marble and cast in bronze to create figures that echo the past but give new life and interpretation to the worlds of ancient Greece and Mexico. Bronze has been used in the 1990s for individual commissions by such artists as John Mills or Evert de Hartogh, while other sculptors, such as Chris Drury, offer copies of small figures either in resin or in bronze.

Modern sculptors are also able to take advantage of modern industrial processes to work in such media as welded copper, stainless steel or Corten steel. New uses have been found for old materials to striking effect, as in the case of Serena de la Hey, who composes her human and animal figures from young willow shoots (withies) interwoven and plaited together, or of Mike Smith, who uses willow wickerwork.

A few firms create reproductions of historical sculptures,

Above left: *'Night and Morning' vase in cast iron by Britannia Iron Works; Swiss Garden, Bedfordshire.* Above right: *Dog of Alcibiades in artificial stone by Austin & Seeley; Blickling Hall, Norfolk.*

Opposite page: *Caryatid in Coade stone; Anglesey Abbey, Cambridgeshire.*

particularly eighteenth-century leadwork. The leading firm is still Crowthers, whose work is often difficult to distinguish from the originals. Lead here is cast in sections in a modified version of the traditional process. Other small firms are returning to the trade.

In the twentieth century ornaments in plastic or plaster have been mass-produced in great numbers; fewer are available in lead, stone and artificial stone (such as Haddonstone). But gardeners looking for garden ornaments or statuary can now, according to their means and inclination, buy original antique items, period reproductions or cheap standard replicas. The continuing interest, at all aesthetic levels, testifies to the enduring appeal of artefacts that give additional character to a garden, whether it is a group of the Three Graces in a grotto or a gnome fishing in a pond.

Left: *The court dwarf Morgante on a tortoise by Cioli; Boboli Gardens, Florence.*

Below: *The Fountain of the Vintage by Cioli; Boboli Gardens, Florence.*

Garden sculpture in Europe

Most garden statuary in Britain is derived from the classical world and the Italian Renaissance, with some influence from seventeenth-century France, also based on classical precedents and myths. The tradition of placing sculpture in gardens goes back at least as far as the ancient Greeks and Romans, for whom displays of sculpture served a number of purposes. One was ostentation, as a tangible expression of having wealth and possessions. Another was to commemorate distinguished contemporaries – heroes, statesmen, emperors. A third purpose was religious – to portray the gods. We know from descriptions and from excavations of such sites as Pompeii that there was sculpture in many Roman gardens and that it could have various meanings. For example, statues of certain readily identified figures, such as Venus, which were understood to exemplify particular attributes, could be taken to personify concepts such as love, justice or peace.

During the Roman Empire (31 BC to AD 330) most Roman sculptures copied Greek originals and were in many cases sculpted by Greeks for their Roman patrons. Sculpture became more naturalistic, more expressive of emotion and more accurate in its delineation of particular people, even though older Greek images were often used as the basis for the pose and Greek symbolism was sometimes continued, such as in the representation of the Emperor Commodus (died 192) as Hercules, a moral hero. In the Casa di Venere at Pompeii there is a painting of a garden with a marble statue whose body is coloured, as well as his draperies, helmet and shield.

The sizes and forms of sculpture varied widely in Roman gardens. In the gardens of Pompeii there were many small figures, usually of white marble but occasionally of bronze, terracotta or coloured marble, in the forms of animals, deities or putti, and herms (heads of Hermes mounted on a tapering column), and small sculpted ornaments such as masks or shields were also found.

In Renaissance Italy a great burgeoning of sculpture followed the rediscovery and new awareness of the relics of antiquity. From the mid fifteenth century ancient artefacts were collected as garden decoration. The future Pope Julius II collected the Apollo Belvedere and many other statues, which became the models for innumerable later copies, and housed them in the Statue Court of the Belvedere at the Vatican. The symbolism and associations of these classical figures were developed and expanded: Hercules was particularly

Above: *Dwarfs on a wall; Villa Valmarana, Italy.*
Below left: *Appennino, or Winter, by Ammanati; Villa Castello, near Florence.*
Below right: *Colossus by Giambologna; Pratolino, Italy.*

Right: *Peasant with a Barrel; Villa Garzoni, Italy.*

Below: *Singerie on the balustrade; Villa Garzoni, Italy.*

identified with gardens, usually in the role of moral hero, while others, such as Vertumnus, Pomona and Priapus, had long been associated with orchards and gardens. In the sixteenth century many more antique sculptures were excavated and then displayed in various private collections. At the same time new sculpture was beginning to produce a canon of figures and symbols that was to dominate western sculpture in future centuries.

Commissioned sculpture was prominent in many Italian gardens of the time. The greatest sculptors – Donatello (1386-1466), Michelangelo (1475-1564), Ammanati (1511-92), Giambologna (1529-1608) – created works for gardens in forms that often harked back to the classical world and might carry a symbolic or associative meaning. Figures were often placed in regular formations in geometrically laid-out gardens or might be found in irregular and Mannerist form in, for example, the enigmatic Florentine grottoes of Boboli or Castello where creatures emerge from the rock walls, stone becoming animate. In this way the sculpture is seen as it is in the process of creation, as with Michelangelo's unfinished slaves, still partly stone blocks, copies of which are in the main grotto at Boboli.

The garden of Boboli, Florence, is a particularly fine sculpture garden. Created in the sixteenth century, when the grottoes came into being, the grounds were expanded considerably in the seventeenth under Grand Dukes Cosimo II and Ferdinando II. There are at present 168 catalogued sculptures in the gardens. There were more originally but several have been removed; some pieces are in the Bargello Museum in the city. Apart from a number of classical Roman originals, the sculptures were made over a period of two hundred years. There is no overall scheme of iconography – or at least none that is easy to discern – but there are set-piece schemes, like the grottoes, which may contain themes and symbolism. Some sculptures are grouped: on the outer ring of the Isolotto there are seventeenth-century Tuscan sculptures in *pietra serena* (local grey stone) of peasants, hunters and other figures in contemporary dress, while opposite each other stand the Game of Saccomazzone, a seventeenth-century piece, and its complement from the late eighteenth century representing the Game of Pentolaccia. There are grotesques, including the court dwarf Morgante as Bacchus naked on the back of a tortoise (1560), deities, musicians, agricultural workers and animals. Group formations often accord with the layout of the gardens – standing around the horseshoe of the amphitheatre, lining the long main axis (the 'Viottolone'), on and around the Isolotto, around the Hemicycle and along the return path past the *limonaia* (lemon house). Thus they emphasise and enhance the geometry of the plan, a function we shall see recurring time and again.

Among the many wonderful Italian gardens that are noted for their sculpture, there are a few especially striking collections of figures. At the Villa d'Este, Tivoli, the sixteenth-century garden created for Cardinal Ippolito d'Este paid tribute to the family through the emblematic figure of Hercules, which stands at the centre of a cross-path between the Grotto of Venus (pleasure/erotic love) and the Grotto of Diana (virtue/chastity). This symbolises the Choice of Hercules, an emblem which recurs in English gardens. Much of the sculpture is related to the astonishing series of water effects such as the Cascades, the Walk of the One Hundred Fountains and the water organ so that, for example, the Dragon fountain, the Owl fountain and the multi-breasted figure of Nature all spout jets of water.

Sculpture often forms part of an architectural showpiece, such as the Water Theatre at Isola Bella on Lake Maggiore. Columns are surmounted by figures, and the tableau has at its peak a rearing unicorn, symbol of the Borromeo family. Mountains or rivers might be commemorated as the sources of land or power or irrigation, or suggest that the owner had tamed them and harnessed them for his purposes. The Medici Villa di Castello is one such, where the family is glorified through an allegorical scheme which displays the four seasons and the local rivers and mountains. For example, the large gaunt old man in bronze, crouching on an islet at the top of the garden, represents the Appennine range or, possibly, Winter. Even more dominant is the colossal figure of the Appennino at Pratolino by Giambologna, so large that it contains two grottoes and one can walk around inside the head.

The most bizarre of all sculpture gardens is Bomarzo. The *sacro bosco* has never been explained totally satisfactorily, and much of its power derives from the sense of enigma and threat of the unknown. Vicino Orsini, the sixteenth-century creator, quotes from, or refers to, various authors such as Ovid, Petrarch and Ariosto, but no single coherent interpretation can now be given. Giants, dragons, the three-headed Cerberus and other terrifying figures populate Bomarzo, which also has an open mouth of Hell. Other figures carry a mixture of meanings ranging from fairly clear to obscure – a tortoise bearing Fame and an elephant with a tower on its back and a dead soldier in its trunk.

Although we tend to associate the formal Italian garden with the Renaissance, the impetus for creating marvels did not die. In the seventeenth and eighteenth centuries the baroque gardens of the Villa Garzoni, Collodi, Tuscany, were made, pure theatre in which the sculpture provides the actors and actresses. Daphne is caught

Above left: *Columbine, Italian; Long Garden, Cliveden, Buckinghamshire.*
Above right: *Term of a faun with grapes by J. Houzeau; Versailles.*

by the sculptor at the moment she is turning into laurel, while many of the terracotta statues are of peasants naturally going about their daily work – one empties a barrel, another tries to control a turkey. The balustrades on the staircases are decorated by *singerie*, monkeys indulging in various antics, such as playing ball games. At one level is a specific green theatre, emphasising the theatrical nature of the whole, with statues of Thalia and Melpomene, the Muses of Comedy and Tragedy, looking out towards the spectator much as Pan and Faun do at Rousham, Oxfordshire. At the highest point is Fame with her trumpet, a suitably flamboyant image with which to crown the garden.

In the baroque period and beyond Venetian sculpture began to predominate. The work of sculptors such as Giovanni and Antonio Bonazza and Orazio Marinali found homes throughout Europe, especially in Germany and Russia, although most was made in the local Venetian stone, which was not very hard-wearing. Good examples also survive in Italian villa gardens in Strà, Padua, Vicenza and Piazzola. Most of the figures are still of classical images – Bacchus, Hercules, Flora, Ceres – though their faces are not always so idealised. But by the eighteenth century there were other important developments. Grotesques became fashionable, as well as figures of *commedia dell'arte* characters such as Harlequin, Columbine and Pantaloon, more familiar to us in porcelain, for example the exquisitely coloured miniatures from Bustelli at Nymphenburg, J. J. Kändler at Meissen and other makers. Four *commedia dell'arte* figures in stone from Padua were bought by Lord Astor for Cliveden, Buckinghamshire, where they stand in the centre of the Long Garden. With them, at the end, are two Venetian figures, also eighteenth-century and attributed to Bonazza, of an allegorical representation of Navigation and of Marco Polo as a Venetian admiral. Dwarf grotesques were known as *gobbi* (dwarves, cripples or hunchbacks) or *Callotti* (after the French engraver of such unfortunates, Jacques Callot) and many were to be found in the Veneto. Villa Valmarana near Vicenza was popularly known as the *Villa ai Nani*, the 'villa with the dwarves'.

In France the garden at Versailles eclipsed all others in its overall splendour and particularly in its sculpture. Although it has largely

Fountain of Bacchus/Autumn by B. & G. Marsy; Versailles.

ceased to have any meaning today, as many statues have been lost or moved from their original positions, the astonishing programme at Versailles was focused on the concept of Louis XIV as the Sun King, with Apollo-centred iconography. A great many facets of life could be brought into the scheme of the sun progressing from dawn to dusk, and the vast number of figures were created by seventy sculptors, working mostly under the king's artistic adviser Charles Le Brun. Most of the figures were classical and some may not now appear to have any discernible connection with the sun programme, but work at Versailles continued over many years and the later sculptures were more for aesthetic effect. Many water features incorporated elaborate fountains and figures representing the principal rivers of France. There were six basic themes, derived from an Italian treatise, *Iconologia,* by Cesare Ripa. These were laid down in the so-called Great Commission of 1674 and were: the Four Elements; the Four Parts of the Day; the Four Parts of the World; the Four Seasons; the Four Humours of Man; the Four Types of Poetry. Although each of these themes offered immense scope, there were in addition a number of sub-themes: the assembly of Olympus, childhood, from war to peace, water, abundance and Apollo versus Dionysus (reason versus passion).

The majority of the Versailles sculptures are of stone but bronze statues feature, especially in the fountains, and there are some lead figures. Those in fountain groups were often gilded or given naturalistic colouring: for example, the Fountain of Bacchus is decorated with luscious-looking purple grapes. A plan of the layout of the gardens indicates the patterning of some of the themes, although over the years that has been considerably confused by the relocation of many figures. However, it is still possible to enjoy the set-piece fountains and groups and to appreciate the clustering of related statues in various spots, particularly in groves which by their names indicate their shape (Star Grove) or theme (Queen's Grove).

Versailles did not have a monopoly of French garden sculpture, though some of it came from the confiscated property of Vaux-le-Vicomte, until that time the greatest of French gardens. Italian influence – and Italian engineers – were behind the grottoes and hydraulic effects at Saint-Germain-en-Laye, and gardens such as Rueil had water and grottoes adorned with squadrons of sculpture. Saint-Cloud had a grand set-piece cascade and basin flanked by sculpture, while the old gardens of Fontainebleau, which contained sculpture placed by earlier monarchs such as Henri IV and François I, were redesigned by Mollet in 1671 to incorporate the existing statuary. From 1700, however, tastes changed: sculpture began to lose

Caricature drummer at Weikersheim, Germany (left), and Child Wrestling with an Infant Satyr at Würzburg, Germany (right).

place even in the formal eighteenth-century gardens and declined further when the pictorial landscape garden came in from England.

From the many separate states that existed before the modern Germany some exceptionally fine and lively figures have come down to us, particularly from the baroque-rococo period. At Schloss Gudenau, near Bonn, a few figures remain from the early eighteenth century which make one wish that more had survived: one of the Seasons is left – Winter, a figure in contemporary costume with fur hat and a huge muff. Similarly, at the Schloss Schönbrunn near Ingolstadt (not to be confused with the Schönbrunn, Vienna) the master of the house had busts of himself and his family set on a wall to represent the Seasons – he is Winter, with fur hat and collar, his wife in a straw bonnet is Summer and his son has a coronet of grapes and other fruit to represent Autumn.

In southern Germany, because of the proximity of Italy, there were examples of *commedia dell'arte* characters and also of *gobbi*. In the Hofgarten at Oettingen near Nördlingen there is a series of dwarf figures which have been moved at various times and probably are fewer in number than originally. The line-up includes a turbaned Turk, a Batavian sailor in breeches and sea-boots, and a dancing-master on one leg. The figures were certainly designed for comic effect. Other *gobbi* at the castle at Weikersheim represent caricatures of members of the court as drummers or gardeners etc, while there

Above left: *Ceres by Ferdinand Tietz; Seehof, Germany.*
Above right: *Diana by Nicholas Stone; Wilton House, Wiltshire.*

Below: *Beasts on poles; Tudor House Museum, Southampton.*

is a dwarf orchestra in the garden of Schloss Sinning, near Neuberg. Many *gobbi* appeared also in Austrian gardens. The cult of the dwarf or grotesque may have given rise to the garden gnome, which came from Germany in the nineteenth century.

Another appealing display of eighteenth-century garden sculpture is the series of children on the balustrades at the Würzburg Residenz. Some are playing games or musical instruments while others fight infant satyrs.

Eighteen *commedia dell'arte* characters feature in the 'comedy parterre' in the gardens of the Schönborn Palace in Vienna, and double that number are in the hedge theatre at Veitshöchheim, sculpted by Ferdinand Tietz. Tietz, born in 1708, was the most gifted sculptor working in Germany in the eighteenth century, and he also produced more than a hundred figures for the gardens of Seehof near Bamberg in 1748-53. Some have a great deal of piquancy and charm, such as the goddess Ceres in an eighteenth-century dress and bonnet. At the Schloss Malberg, Eifel, there is a terrace balustrade adorned with six rococo figures by Tietz from the 1750s and a further four on the wall of the Round Garden below. While based on the classics, Ovid's *Metamorphoses* in particular, they have a playfulness that would not have been encountered earlier. Unusually there are both male and female Pans. The figures are made from sandstone and were originally polychrome.

The superb rococo garden of Veitshöchheim contains well over three hundred sculptures (modern copies) on all manner of subjects – allegorical, classical, the Seasons – and of contemporary courtiers and other persons. The centrepiece is a basin to glorify the arts, created by Tietz in 1765-6, which has a Mount Parnassus in the middle with Pegasus at the top. At Herrenhausen, Hanover, a late seventeenth-century baroque layout includes an embroidered parterre garden with thirty-two figures and a hedge theatre with gilded lead representations of the family of the Electors of Hanover in classical poses. Hellbrunn, Salzburg, was an early seventeenth-century garden heavily under the Italian Mannerist influence, with grottoes, strange forms (a lion man), animals and trick fountains. Schwetzingen is a pictorial, eighteenth-century templescape around a formal embroidered parterre containing, among other things, the Von Verschaffelt Stag Fountain. Finally may be mentioned the stupendous water garden at Wilhelmshöhe, Hessen, planned in the eighteenth century but not completed. The upper series of grottoes, fountains and cascades was crowned by a large Octagon reservoir, surmounted by a version of the Farnese Hercules, which therefore looked down from the highest point in the garden.

Tudor and Elizabethan

Although there was so much garden sculpture in Italy in the sixteenth century, its influence was hardly felt in Tudor and Elizabethan England. While there was more emphasis on gardens as places of pleasure and elaborate design than in previous centuries, especially in the royal gardens of display, in terms of sculpture two native traditions predominated in a number of the great gardens of the time, the heraldic and the emblematic. Hampton Court was the supreme heraldic garden. Henry VIII acquired the palace from Wolsey in 1525 and developed the estate over the next twenty or so years. Heraldry was prominent and dominant, taking the form of creatures in wood – the King's Beasts – painted and gilded, and usually set on top of slender columns or poles. The beasts represented the great families of the past converging to produce the Tudor dynasty. They appeared in the Privy Orchard, the Privy Garden, the Pond Garden and the Mount Garden; the path circling up the Mount was decorated by beasts in stone, including dragons, greyhounds and a griffin. For a detailed account the reader is referred to Sir Roy Strong's *The Renaissance Garden in England.*

In the Privy Orchard there were initially seven beasts: a bill for January 1531 mentions two dragons, two greyhounds, one lion, one horse and one antelope, each costing eighteen shillings. They stood on poles painted white, or green and white (the Tudor colours), and each held a small flag bearing the royal arms or the Tudor rose. Later were added three antelopes, three dragons, three lions, two harts, two greyhounds and three hinds. Coats of arms and heraldic devices, displayed on pennants, banners, shields and badges of various sorts, had been widely used in the late medieval period, and their spread into the garden indicated not only the King's power but also the inherited sources of power.

The Privy Garden had no fewer than 159 King's (and Queen's) Beasts, this time at twenty shillings each. Unfortunately there are no good visual records of this, but from a sketch at a distance by Van Wyngaerde, *c.*1555, we can see them in serried rows along walks and railings.

The Royal Palace of Whitehall was another palace Henry VIII took over from his former chancellor. By 1545 the Great Garden had been laid out, with more than a nod in the direction of Hampton Court. Once again there were the wooden poles or columns surmounted by carved animals, their horns gilded, bearing flags on upright staves. Two views of *c.*1545 show raised beds, railings in green and white, as at Hampton Court, and four of the beasts, identified by Sir Roy Strong as Edward III's griffin, the Beaufort yale (a hoofed and horned monster), the Richmond white greyhound and possibly a white hind. The depiction of just these four figures (out of thirty-four) is no doubt significant and emphasises the particular Tudor family and dynastic connotations.

The third great garden was at Nonsuch Palace, near Cheam, Surrey, which was unfinished when Henry VIII died in 1547. Although the basic layout of the gardens had been completed by then, they were brought to the fullness of their fame and maturity only after 1556, through the work of Henry, twelfth Earl of Arundel, and his son-in-law, John, Lord Lumley. The two-storey Banqueting House can be dated from Henry VIII's time, for the King's Beasts adorned the roof. However, under Arundel and Lumley a Tudor heraldic garden was turned into a composite of Italian Mannerist allegory and Elizabethan emblem. The Italian element entered as a result of a period Lumley spent in Italy. This manifested itself in the form of classical mythology, particularly the theme of Diana. A key area was the Grove of Diana, a clearing with a rock fountain and a sculpture of the story of Diana and Actaeon. Further, the Banqueting House became known as the Temple of Diana. There was also a fountain of Diana adjacent to the house. The symbolism of Diana could be read with the standard Renaissance interpretation of the story of the goddess and Actaeon given a moral: since he was torn to death by his own hounds for daring to spy on Diana bathing, we should learn from this to control our passions.

But at Nonsuch the theme had a further purpose. Diana was also identified with Queen Elizabeth I. The goddess is a complicated symbol, representing the huntress, the moon, motherhood and chastity, and her attributes were perceived to be those of the Queen (chastity, mother of her people). At Nonsuch this was reinforced by two other emblems, the pelican and the phoenix. An arch near the Temple of Diana bore both figures, while there was a veined marble fountain on top of which was the pelican in her piety, pecking her breast to feed her young with her own blood. This was a symbol which came to be closely associated with Elizabeth, meaning that she sacrificed herself to serve her country, and it figures (for example in jewellery) in portraits of the Queen. The phoenix was likewise identified with her.

At Nonsuch the old heraldic forms were still used, but for Lumley family purposes. Instead of many wooden columns there was a small number of marble columns: two black pillars framed the Diana fountain, on top of which was the device of the Lumleys, the popinjay.

More popinjays acting as spouts decorated the table fountain outside the south front of the palace. By the south-east tower the leaping white horse of Arundel stood on another marble column, matched by a tall obelisk of veined marble by the south-west tower bearing Lumley's coat of arms.

During Elizabeth's reign the impetus for garden making passed from the crown to influential courtiers. Often, as with Nonsuch, the earlier heraldic tradition would be used for personal purpose: at Kenilworth, the central fountain was decorated with the Earl of Leicester's device, a bear with a ragged staff. Many great houses would offer hospitality to the Queen on her tours of the country, and it was diplomatic to make some reference to her in the house or gardens, as at Theobalds, Hertfordshire, where Sir Robert Cecil laid out a series of knot quarters where each knot carried appropriate symbolism.

None of these magnificent gardens has survived in its original form. For modern representations of the heraldic form of sculpture one must turn to the creation by Sylvia Landsberg of a Tudor-style garden, complete with beasts on poles, at the Tudor House Museum, Southampton. The beasts in stone outside the Palm House at Kew Gardens, Surrey, dating from 1956, are copies by the original sculptor of the Queen's Beasts, which had been designed to go outside Westminster Abbey for the coronation of Elizabeth II in 1953.

Taste (left) and Juno (right) by C. G. Cibber; Belvoir, Leicestershire.

The seventeenth century

Lumley's Nonsuch may have provided a solitary example of the Italian garden in its day, but the scene was very different in the era following Queen Elizabeth's death in 1603. Through the connections of the Stuart court Britain was exposed to the influence of both French and Italian formal garden design, and even such Italian wonders as have been mentioned were copied, and sometimes surpassed. Through the work in particular of Salomon de Caus, the world of the Italian grotto with its accompaniment of automata, *giochi d'acqua* (water jokes) and other hydraulic effects now became available to his English patrons. De Caus (1576-1626), a Huguenot working in England, had been to Italy and was familiar with gardens such as Pratolino and Villa d'Este. He designed the gardens of Greenwich Palace and Somerset House, London, for Queen Anne (wife of James I) and those of Richmond Palace, Surrey, for Henry, Prince of Wales, although work ceased on Henry's death in 1612. Unfortunately this prevented the completion of garden features on a staggering scale. One of them seems to have been made, but there is a surprising lack of description of it, and it may not have lasted long. It seems that de Caus designed a giant three times as large as the Colossus at Pratolino, with several rooms inside, a dovecote in the head and grottoes in the base. He drew a number of sketches for such gigantic figures, some with automata performing in the grottoes inside.

At Somerset House de Caus designed a rock island fountain representing Mount Parnassus, with four river gods to denote the main rivers of Britain. This served as a demonstration both of hydraulics and of statue making and as a tribute to the Queen. The Parnassus fountain group had a cavern on one side in which the nine Muses sat with instruments appropriate to their characters. At the very top was a gilded figure of Pegasus. Once again the original model was at Pratolino, but de Caus's creation far eclipsed its inspiration.

The gardens at Greenwich included a grotto aviary and an elaborate fountain in the centre of the garden, this time in the form of a gilded female figure pouring water from a cornucopia. De Caus also worked, more briefly, for Robert Cecil at Hatfield House, Hertfordshire, where he built a fountain composed of a rock with a figure painted to simulate copper.

In the 1620s de Caus's younger brother Isaac created the grotto lined with shells and rockwork inside the house at Woburn Abbey,

Bedfordshire, where it may still be seen. During the following decade he worked for the fourth Earl of Pembroke at Wilton House, Wiltshire, where he laid out a magnificent Italianate garden with embroidered parterres, a wilderness, a water parterre, an amphitheatre and a grotto, inside which were characteristic elaborate de Caus effects: figures that wept water, the imitated sound of birdsong, and water jokes. In the garden there were 'coronet fountains', where a ball with a crown on top was supported on a rusticated column and jets of water played on the crown to make it revolve. At Wilton the stone fountain sculptures were by the Devon-born Nicholas Stone (*c.*1587-1647) and they have survived, though relocated in the front court: Venus and Cupid, Susanna pulling a thorn from her foot, Diana and Cleopatra. The sculptural themes appear to have been of love and chastity. Further out, among the groves, were statues of Flora and Bacchus and, beyond, an oval area in which stood a copy of the Borghese gladiator by Hubert le Sueur (*c.*1580 to *c.*1670), who brought casts and moulds from Italy and created a number of bronze copies of various antique sculptures. In the water parterre at Wilton there were also fountains and individual figures: one sculpture of a female by Stone has survived. The cascade was surmounted by a figure of Pegasus. Sir Roy Strong has suggested a possible allegorical scheme of the gardens.

Stone's work also featured in the gardens of Sir John Danvers at Chelsea, London. Coloured figures of a gardener and his wife, attired appropriately, were very early examples of the naturalistic, contemporary representations that were to become common in the following century. Two pairs of figures, Hercules and Antaeus, and Cain and Abel, were sited at the ends of the walks near the house. It is possible that these have survived, for the corresponding figures (also in stone) are to be found today at St Paul's Walden Bury (see page 46), where they have been attributed to John Van Nost. (This is unlikely since his garden works were generally in lead.) Stone also produced six statues of shepherds and shepherdesses. Such figures equate with an idyllic world of love and pastoral life as expressed in the poetry of Spenser and the masques of Ben Jonson and Inigo Jones.

The early seventeenth century saw the rise of the concept of the garden as a sculpture gallery or display of ancient sculptures. Arundel House in London had Italian-style terraces and galleries to display the Earl of Arundel's collection of 128 busts, thirty-two statues and many other pieces. Meanwhile André Mollet, in laying out the grounds at St James's Palace, London, set aside a museum garden for Charles I's considerable collection of sculpture.

Father Time by C. G. Cibber; Belton, Lincolnshire.

The gardens of Somerset House, made originally for James I's queen, as we have seen, were altered by Queen Henrietta Maria, wife of Charles I, to include a number of fountains and statues that subsequently found homes elsewhere. Lucy Harington created the famous gardens of Moor Park, Hertfordshire, in 1617-27 with eight statues in the formal parterres near the house and rockwork and fountains in the wilderness at a distance at a lower level.

If Nicholas Stone was the greatest sculptor of garden figures in England in the first half of the seventeenth century, Caius Gabriel Cibber (1630-1700) was certainly the most important in the latter part of the century. He was born in Denmark but had made his way to England before the Restoration and was employed in the workshop of John Stone, son of Nicholas. He worked extensively in monumental and tomb sculpture but produced some memorable pieces in a number of gardens, with stylistic echoes of Holland and Italy (where he had studied). The fullest display of his garden art today is at Belvoir, Leicestershire, where he made four Seasons, two Senses and a Juno, which have been moved to a slope slightly reminiscent of the arrangement in the Vale of Venus at Rousham (page 49). The contract, dated 1680, was for the seven statues, identified as above, at £35 each. They were carved from stone from the Ketton quarries not far away. It is a slightly strange collection: the Seasons are identifiable by their attributes (sheaf of corn, grapes etc), but why are there only two Senses and why is Juno by herself? Juno is represented with her peacock, but Smell could be mistaken for Diana, with her dog, and Taste has a basket of fruit, which might be appropriate, but an ape squats menacingly at her feet and

Flora by C. G. Cibber; Chatsworth, Derbyshire.

a Medusa mask snarls out from each side of the plinth. The draperies run counter to the pose in some cases, a Cibber trademark. The plinths are as noteworthy as the figures themselves, with carved swags, coats of arms and masks.

Cibber produced a bagpiper, now in the Victoria and Albert Museum, and a series of sculptures for the Earl of Kingston at Thoresby, Nottinghamshire, but from these only a sphinx remains. His Father Time at Belton, Lincolnshire, comprises a sundial supported by figures of Time and a cherub. His greatest work in gardens was at Chatsworth, Derbyshire, but so much has gone that Belvoir is the best place to see his garden sculpture. However, Cibber's powerful Triton fountain – Triton surrounded by sea-horses – is still at Chatsworth, fed by the great cascade. Some of his figures have been moved into the house, such as Apollo and Pallas Athene on the staircase. In the gardens a pair of sphinxes remain, and possibly one or two other figures, such as Flora in the Rose Garden. Cibber was also employed by Wren at Hampton Court in the 1690s, but the statues have been dispersed or are difficult to identify. Two great urns were modelled by him, one of the Triumph of Bacchus, which has been moved to the east front, and the other of Meleager and the Boar, which is now in the Orangery at Kensington Palace, London.

There has been much notable statuary at Hampton Court, though it has had a confusing history over the years as many items have been moved, both within the grounds and elsewhere altogether. The Arethusa fountain, for example, arrived from Somerset House in 1655-6 and was installed in the Privy Garden, only to be removed in 1701 when the garden was re-laid. In 1713-14 it crossed the road to Bushy Park, its present home. The two urns by Cibber were paired with two others by Edward Pearce (or Pierce), and then both pairs were moved. In 1659 the Privy Garden contained

Above left: *Apollo Looking at the Sun, Italian; Privy Garden, Hampton Court, Middlesex.* Above right: *Vulcan at his Anvil, copy of Italian original; Privy Garden, Hampton Court, Middlesex.*

two bronze statues (Venus and Cleopatra) and two in white marble (Adonis and Apollo). All had disappeared by 1695. The new Privy Garden of 1702 contained five marble statues from Italy: Apollo Looking at the Sun, Vulcan, Apollo with Marsyas, Ceres and Bacchus. These, and practically all the statuary, were taken by George IV to Windsor in 1829. In the restoration of the Privy Garden, completed in 1995, Apollo Looking at the Sun is back in its original place, while the other four have been replaced in white Carrara marble since the originals were too damaged by weather to keep outdoors.

In 1701 four bronze figures appeared in the fountain parterre. One was certainly a Gladiator, from St James's Park, another a Diana; the third was described as Apollo but was actually Antinous, and the fourth was Hercules, though there is a puzzling later reference to a different figure, Saturn, about to eat one of his children. It was Hercules, however, who was removed to Windsor in 1829, where he still stands.

Towards the end of the century lead casting was introduced from the Low Countries and sculptors swiftly changed to this medium, not least because of the opportunities it offered to make several copies of a statue from a single original. One of the first was Arnold Quellin (1653-86), who came from a family of sculptors from Antwerp and was in England by the late 1670s. He set up a workshop in which the great garden sculptor in lead, John Van Nost (died 1710), also Flemish, learnt his trade, although he may have acquired some knowledge of lead casting before he came to England. Quellin himself did not undertake garden commissions, and Van Nost, in England from about 1678, originally worked in marble for many of his monumental pieces, only later branching out into garden sculpture. Van Nost became Quellin's foreman and after Quellin's death married his widow. Although some of his garden figures date from the end of the seventeenth century we shall treat him as the first of the eighteenth-century lead sculptors.

Cupid and the Hornet's Nest by John Van Nost the Elder; Melbourne Hall, Derbyshire.

The early eighteenth century

The early years of the eighteenth century were dominated by two names: Van Nost and Carpenter. Unfortunately the first name conceals more than one person (there were three John Van Nosts for a start) and this has caused a great deal of confusion. John Van Nost the Elder, who died in August 1710, created many lead figures which were to become standard throughout the century and were often copied. His work can be seen at its finest at Melbourne Hall, Derbyshire, and at Rousham, with other pieces at Wilton, Hampton Court and possibly Powis Castle, Powys. He had as his assistant Andries Carpentière (later anglicised to Andrew Carpenter), among others. It is difficult now to determine in all cases whether pieces should be attributed to Van Nost or to Carpenter, who later set up on his own account and may have used some of Van Nost's models.

After Van Nost's death the business was taken over by his cousin John, also a good sculptor, who was responsible for the equestrian figure of George I at Stowe, Buckinghamshire, and also provided figures for Canons Ashby (Northamptonshire), Wrest Park (Bedfordshire), Castle Bromwich (West Midlands) and other places. Again, some of the models may have been taken from the elder Van Nost's yard. In April 1729 this second John Van Nost died, and his widow took over. Their son, John the third, had worked at the yard and had been apprenticed to the sculptor Henry Scheemakers in 1726. By 1734 the business was in the hands of another relative, Anthony Van Nost, who retained it until it was bought by John Cheere in 1737. John the third moved to Dublin *c.*1750 and met with great success there. He died in 1780, aged about seventy. For good measure John Van Nost the Elder is said to have had a nephew, Gerard, who was also a sculptor.

The auction sale catalogue of 17th April 1712, when 140 items from Van Nost's collection were offered following his death in 1710, survives. There was a reserve or starting price on all items, and both marble and lead pieces were on offer, the former including tables and chimney pieces. Among the garden sculpture, apart from vases and fountain figures, were a shepherd and dog, a shepherdess and lamb, a shepherd piping, the Four Seasons, a fox, two Cupids fighting, two Cupids kissing, the Farnese Hercules, Cain and Abel after 'John de Bellone' (Giambologna), Adonis, Flora, Bacchus, Ceres, Pan, Faunus, a dancing nymph, Diana with a buck, a satyr, a sundial, a young Bacchus, a dancing boy and a standing boy.

Many of these figures are identifiable not only with Van Nost's known work at Rousham, Melbourne Hall and elsewhere, but with John the second's commissions and Carpenter's too. Even where Van Nost had received a specific commission, like the pairs of Cupids (for Melbourne) it appears that he reused the models to replicate the figures. Some images, such as the shepherd-piper, were reproduced for years to come, some with variations, copying rather than using the actual original model.

The Van Nost yard was in Hyde Park Road and this area became well-known for a number of statuaries who set up business there, offering a range of statues for sale or working to commission. One of them was Andrew Carpenter (1670s-1737), the elder Van Nost's chief assistant, who started his own yard in Portugal Row just off Hyde Park Road. He supplied figures for Powis Castle, Stowe, Castle Howard (North Yorkshire), Wrest Park, Studley Royal (North Yorkshire), Ditchley (Oxfordshire) and Canons (Middlesex), but several of these appear to be identifiable with works known to have been originated by Van Nost. What he probably supplied was a mixture of original work plus copies from moulds or models from the Van Nost business. Among lesser sculptors producing leadwork from premises around Hyde Park were Edward Hurst, who supplied a shepherd and shepherdess in 1718 for Charlecote Park, Warwickshire (see illustration), Thomas Manning, who had worked for Van Nost the Elder and later set up several yards, and Richard Osgood, who produced figures for Chatsworth in the 1690s, did much repair work at Hampton Court and continued until the late 1720s. His Samson and the Philistine group – often described as Cain and Abel – was moved from its first home to Chiswick and then joined his other work at Chatsworth. Osgood was responsible for the statuary at Denham Place, Buckinghamshire, which included

Shepherd by Edward Hurst; Charlecote Park, Warwickshire.

two military figures on top of the gate piers (1694), several statues in a formal sculpture garden and a series of dancing boys the whole length of a long wall.

When he commissioned a statue a patron would often have his own agenda, which might extend beyond the purchase of mere decoration. For example, Van Nost's work for William III at Hampton Court around 1700 included not only repairs, vases, pedestals and the boys with baskets of fruit which stood on top of the gate piers (we see two today), but Portland stone panels for piers fronting the gravel walk, 'two carved with the King's arms, two with laurel branches, sword, sceptre and crown'. This emblematic approach was carried further by a design for a statue of the King on a pedestal flanked by two children representing the continents of Europe and America. William is garbed as a Roman emperor and stands in a pose of domination over the two small figures, illustrating the might and power of the king. This was not executed, though the intention seems to have been to have a statue of the King replacing Diana at the top of the fountain at the end of a grand tree-lined avenue. Van Nost did, however, make two kneeling figures in lead, an Indian and a Negro, bearing sundials, which might also represent the continents of Asia and Africa and have connotations of submission. They were placed briefly in the Privy Garden and then moved. Van Nost drew a number of designs for the Diana fountain, or parts of it, and also designed or made a number of statues, though much of his work was halted by the King's death in 1702.

Van Nost created a large number of statues at Melbourne Hall for Thomas Coke, who had inherited the estate in 1696. The four pairs of amorini, variously interpreted as Castor and Pollux or Eros and his brother Anteros, tell a story of a fight and eventual reconciliation and are derived from Annibale Carracci's ceiling scenes in the gallery of the Farnese Palace, Rome. They seem to have caused trouble in the execution: Van Nost told Coke as early as 1699 that he had 'set up two models of boys but they were not to my mind' and the commission was not completed until payment in August 1706 for the four groups. In addition to these enchanting little figures, there were also single Cupids: one, for instance, shapes his bow while another is stung by hornets. A similar series is at Wilton. Among other small creations at Melbourne are Triton and his companions in the two small fountains in the woods. Larger works included the Mercury after Giambologna and the pair of Perseus (£25) and Andromeda (£20), originally painted white to resemble stone. These, too, are based on Carracci but Andromeda

Vase of the Seasons by John Van Nost the Elder; Melbourne Hall, Derbyshire.

is reversed as if Van Nost had taken it from a reverse-image engraving. Perseus holds up the severed head of Medusa in triumph. Also at Melbourne is a pairing of the Hampton Court figures, so familiar and copied, the kneeling Indian and Blackamoor, this time supporting urns rather than sundials. They were painted black with coloured sashes and cost £30 each.

The highlight at Melbourne is the wonderful Vase of the Seasons, positioned at the central rondpoint of the wood. Van Nost received £100 for it in 1705. The vase stands on a stone base and is supported by four monkeys. The body of the vase depicts amorini or children playing, and above are the Four Seasons, their heads standing above the rim of the vase. On top is a basket filled with fruit. The modelling is intricate and exceptionally elaborate and is one of the triumphs of leadwork. The basket corresponds with those on top of the gate piers at Hampton Court. A similar vase, with minor variations and a fox on top, was bought by Charles Hamilton for Painshill, Surrey, but is now at Syon House, Middlesex.

Van Nost offered Coke a range of further figures, including Hercules and Antaeus, and a Sabine rape, which may be the statue of which Hamilton purchased a copy later on. At about the same time he supplied General Dormer with lead statues for Rousham, the most striking of which are Pan and Faun in Venus's Vale. Although these were purchased at the beginning of the century it was not until the 1730s that William Kent worked at Rousham to create the gardens that we know today, which make such telling use of Van Nost's pieces. The sculpture programme at Rousham is described in the following chapter.

The leadwork at Powis Castle could be by either Van Nost or Carpenter, or shared between them. The equestrian figure of Fame, dramatically blowing her trumpet, is signed by Carpenter, but that does not prove the authorship of all the pieces. It was originally part of a fountain at the foot of the terraces, with a jet of water coming through the trumpet. Like many of the figures, it was made from local lead. Along the balustrade of one of the terraces are three (formerly four) figures of great charm – shepherds and shepherdesses with a dog and a lamb, playing the bagpipes. They were originally coloured to look like stone. On the lower (Orangery) level there was a young Faun; and a peacock survives, brought to Powis by Lord Clive from his other seat at Claremont in Surrey. An unusual item is the Hercules killing the many-headed Hydra: Hercules is in lead, while the Hydra is of local stone. The

Below left: *Samson and the Philistine by John Van Nost the Elder; Anglesey Abbey, Cambridgeshire.*
Below right: *Shepherd-piper by John Van Nost the Elder or Andrew Carpenter; Powis Castle, Powys.*

representation of Hercules with club raised aloft is found in other places, such as on the terrace at Goldney, Bristol.

The rusticity of the balustrade figures is matched elsewhere in the early eighteenth century. Wrest Park had figures of haymakers and gardeners with rakes and scythes as well as the figures we see there today, provided by Carpenter, John Van Nost the Second and John Cheere. Carpenter's figure of William III stands in front of Archer's pavilion terminating the canal view. Rustic characters (see also the pair at Charlecote, page 36) might wear either contemporary or classical costume, with an increasing tendency to the former.

A great deal of statuary was ordered for Castle Howard, and it is tempting to seek a coherent programme, but in the end it appears that Lord Carlisle simply acquired the best of what was available. In any case the sculpture came in two phases: Carpenter supplied a number of pieces in 1723 and John Cheere provided some at a later date. According to George Vertue, Carpenter was a 'gross, heavy man' but was 'in his time esteemed for his skill and made many works for noblemen and others of distinction'. His yard was successful at first, but Vertue considered that later on 'he had much ado to hold up his head', as a result of being undersold and having to lower his prices. Carpenter sent a stock list to Lord Carlisle, from which he chose the Farnese Hercules, the 'Spartan Boys', sitting Venus (probably confused with Spinario) and Faunus. All except the Boys (also known as the Wrestlers) survive, Hercules along the terrace walk, Spinario at the end of the formal garden, and Faunus with a kid near the house. The Wrestlers are identifiable with the group at Studley Royal, also attributed to Carpenter. The catalogue includes a number of standard figures – an Indian, a bagpiper, Cain and Abel, Apollo, Adonis, Flora, the Seasons – which are common to Van Nost's list and suggest that Carpenter took over many of his models.

Carpenter is known to have supplied figures for Wrest Park, Ickworth (Suffolk), Purley Hall (Berkshire) and Briggens (Hertfordshire). Whether his work at Studley Royal comprised more than the Wrestlers is hard to determine, since other lead figures have been repositioned and have been replaced by different figures over the years. The Neptune may, however, be the one in his catalogue. He may also have produced some figures for Chatsworth, such as the Faun with kid which is similar to the one at Castle Howard, but Van Nost the Elder is known to have worked at Chatsworth. Carpenter was paid by Lord Burlington for minor work at Chiswick and also produced a kneeling Blackamoor *c.*1735 for

Above: *Father Time in stone; Duncombe Park, North Yorkshire.*

Right: *Pan by John Van Nost the Elder; Rousham, Oxfordshire.*

Above left: *King William III, attributed to Andrew Carpenter; Wrest Park, Bedfordshire.*
Above right: *King George I by John Van Nost the Younger; Stowe, Buckinghamshire.*

Dunham Massey, Cheshire, which is rather differently modelled from others such as at Arley Hall, Cheshire, which stem from Van Nost the Elder's work for Hampton Court and Melbourne Hall.

The placing of sculpture in early eighteenth-century gardens was a matter of much concern: correctness was earnestly advocated. Thus, Stephen Switzer comments in *Ichnographia Rustica* (1718): 'It cann't but be an unpleasant Sight (as common as it is) to view *Jupiter, Mars, Neptune*, and the rest of the capital Deities of Heaven, misplac'd ..... Others, perhaps, err in another respect, by placing *Pan* as a Tutelar God in the Flower-Garden, whilst *Ceres* and *Flora* are the silent Inhabitants of Woods and Groves. To this may be often join'd an Impropriety in the Gesture and Habiliments of these Gods, which ought to differ, as the Actions they are representing do.' He then goes on to explain how the statues should be disposed: '*Jupiter* and *Mars* should possess the largest Open Centres and Lawns of a grand Design, elevated upon Pedestal Columnial ..... *Neptune* should possess the Centre of the greatest body of Water, (be it either Fountain, Bason, or whatever of that kind) in his Chariot, attended by the *Naiades*, *Tritons*, and other his Sea-Attendants.'

In his *New Principles of Gardening* (1728) Batty Langley follows a similar line: 'There is nothing adds so much to the Beauty and Grandeur of Gardens, as fine Statues; and nothing more disagreeable, than when wrongly plac'd; as *Neptune* on a Terrace-Walk, Mount &c. or *Pan*, the God of Sheep, in a large Basin, Canal, or Fountain.' He lists areas of a garden with suggested sculpture: open lawns (Mars, Jupiter, Venus, Apollo, the Muses, Hercules etc), woods and groves (Actaeon, Philomela, and Ceres and Flora, though disapproved of by Switzer), water (Neptune etc), orchards (Pomona), flower gardens (Flora, Venus, Diana, Daphne), vineyards (Bacchus), mounts (Aeolus), places for banqueting (Comus). These are the main names; Langley also suggests a great many minor and, to most people today, obscure deities.

In general these principles were followed, not only in sculpture but in buildings dedicated to figures in the classical pantheon: thus the Temple of Aeolus at Kew, Surrey, is on top of a mount, and the Temple of Comus was the name bestowed on one of the supper-

Below left: *Hercules (Farnese) by Andrew Carpenter; Castle Howard, North Yorkshire.*
Below right: *Silenus with the Infant Bacchus by Andrew Carpenter; Castle Howard, North Yorkshire.*

box semicircles at Vauxhall pleasure gardens, London. Nor were considerations of propriety confined to classical sculpture. James Ralph in his *Critical Review* of 1734 extends the principle to all statuary: 'In the first place, therefore, a statue should be good in itself; in the next, it should be erected to advantage; and, lastly, it should, in its own nature, be suited to the place. To compleat an area, end a vesta [vista], adorn a fountain, or decorate a banquetting-house or alcove, is the just and natural use of statues: not to people a garden, and make a nuisance of what ought to be a beauty.'

Ralph was severely condemnatory of what he saw in the leadmakers' yards: 'Between this and *Hyde-Park-Corner*, there is nothing more remarkable, except the shops and yards of the *Statuaries*; and sorry I am that they afford a judicious foreigner such flagrant opportunities to arraign and condemn our taste. Among a hundred statues, you shall not see one even tolerable, either in design or execution; nay, even the copies of the antique are so monstrously wretched, that one can hardly guess at their originals.' Ralph puts the blame not on the makers but on the buyers who first make a wrong choice and then 'resolve to purchase their follies as cheap as possible': a harsh judgement, and one that was shared by J. T. Smith a hundred years later, looking back to 'the despicable manufactory' of the Van Nost/Cheere yard and recording that, although the original sources were of the finest, the 'leaden productions, although they found numerous admirers and purchasers, were never countenanced by men of true taste; for it is well known, that when applications were made to the Earl of Burlington for his sanction, he always spoke of them with sovereign contempt, observing that the uplifted arms of leaden figures, in consequence of the pliability and weight of the material, would in course of time appear little better than crooked billets.' This could not have been entirely so, however, for Burlington commissioned a number of lead pieces for Chiswick, including sphinxes of high quality.

It may be the case that copies of well-known classical or Renaissance originals were sometimes remote from the quality of the original but, after a space of 250 years or more, modern opinion is more likely to find charm in the productions of the time, and to enjoy the patina and weathering of lead, even though the pristine colouring and effect may have been lost. It is also likely that the better pieces have generally survived, for a great deal of leadwork was melted down for the American War of Independence, and items of lesser quality were presumably the first to be sacrificed.

The sculpture programmes

While there was a concern about the appropriateness of the location of classical figures in the eighteenth century, sometimes an attempt was made to make a broader programme of associations or iconography, so that the statuary had to be 'read' for its meaning. Most displays of garden sculpture are ornamental rather than meaningful, but in one or two gardens there was a definite programme and in some others it may not be fanciful to detect points being made by particular pieces.

Iconography was not new in British gardens. We have noted possible schemes at Wilton and at Sir John Danvers's house in Chelsea, both in the seventeenth century, and some Renaissance emblems and meanings were carried on into the eighteenth. Cesare Ripa's *Iconologia*, which was used as a source at Versailles and elsewhere, had been published in Rome in 1593 and was widely translated throughout Europe. In England the first edition was not until 1709, which is unexpectedly late for Renaissance symbolism to make an appearance, yet it seems to have been popular reading and was still being used in 1779, when George Richardson's *Iconography, or A Collection of Emblematical Figures, Moral and Instructive* came out. This expanded Ripa by the addition of material from Egyptian, Greek and Roman sources. Images covered the elements, celestial bodies, the seasons and months of the year, the hours of the day, the continents, the principal rivers, the four ages, the Muses, the senses, arts, sciences, dispositions, faculties, virtues and vices; over 420 categories or images in all. Some of these categories were represented in sculpture, usually with the appropriate attribute, such as Fame with her trumpet. But although we find Ripaean emblems in some gardens, the force of their emblematic meaning tends to be muted, whereas contemporary associations and the meanings attached to classical figures seem to have exerted more power over British imaginations.

John Aislabie retreated in disgrace to Studley Royal, North Yorkshire, following the collapse of the South Sea Bubble in 1720-1. Patrick Eyres (see 'Further Reading') views Studley as a statement of the contrast between private pleasure and civic duty (*privitas* and *civitas*), first announced by the two heads of Janus at the entrance gate, one dignified, the other a leering Pan. Some of the statuary can be read in such a scheme and in the context of Aislabie's career: the Hercules and Antaeus in stone may represent reason conquering the passions or more specifically Aislabie triumphing over those

Left: *Hercules and Antaeus; Studley Royal, North Yorkshire.*

Right: *Hercules; St Paul's Walden Bury, Hertfordshire.*

who would have had him arraigned for treason. There were originally a number of sculptures with erotic overtones, none more so than the Priapus (long since vanished) near the Banqueting House. Other figures, such as the contending Wrestlers, also suggest a struggle: again, Aislabie against his enemies or in general terms pleasure versus duty. Venus was to be found in the Banqueting House and Pan (also lost) continued a theme which encompassed the erotic, the natural and the rural.

Although Castle Howard may not have an overall sculpture programme, one particular area, Wray Wood, seems to have had a Garden of Rustic Delights and Erotic Love. On this wooded hill beside the house there were, early in the eighteenth century, an Apollo, a Bacchus and a Venus, with a lawn in a clearing adorned with lead figures of a satyr ravishing a nymph, Diana holding a buck by the horn and a shepherd and his dog, all painted white.

At St Paul's Walden Bury, laid out by Edward Gilbert in the

1720s in a basic goose-foot design (where the allées slope up and down), there is a series of figures that have been interpreted as conflict leading to resolution. However, some of the figures are of later date than others, so the scheme may be accidental or at any rate not devised at any particular date. On the house lawn are two stone groups previously attributed to Van Nost but which might possibly be Nicholas Stone's figures for the Danvers garden in Chelsea. They are certainly in conflict – Hercules struggling with Antaeus and Samson slaying the Philistine. Not far away on a cross path is a Cain and Abel group in lead, with equally brutal theme. Resolution there may be in the form of a triumphant Hercules in the Farnese pose with a club, halfway along the central allée. Other figures, such as John Cheere's group of Charity, date from much later in the century.

At Rousham there is an elaborate scheme that relates not only to the choice of figures and their positioning but also to their materials. On the top walk from the Bowling Green the visitor is led from the Lion Attacking the Horse, on the main axis from the house, via a term identifiable as Minerva, to the Dying Gladiator. All are of stone, whereas the figures in the lower garden are of lead. The Lion Attacking the Horse, by Scheemakers, is similar to a group in the 'Little Rome' tableau at the Villa d'Este, where the lion represents Rome. Scheemakers' version, however, is based on an adaptation by Giambologna, who created a number of versions in bronze. Minerva represents not only wisdom, suggesting a sacred circuit that both gives and requires knowledge and understanding, but also war, which continues the military theme, while the Dying Gladiator, also by Scheemakers, is a casualty of conflict. Both Scheemakers' figures signify the power and influence of Rome, expressed in an aggressive and militaristic way, contrasting with rural classicism in the gardens below. At the Dying Gladiator there is a balustrade (concealing the Praeneste arcade underneath, which is visible only from the lower path) at the ends of which are two terms, Hercules and Pan, as if to suggest the boundary between heroism and rural retreat. Hercules, indeed, embraces both and stands aptly at the junction.

A little further along the top walk a Palladian gateway is encountered, with two niches containing lead figures of Flora and Plenty. These embody the themes of nature's abundance that are taken up later. Together with the pediment of the gateway, a triangle is formed, another grouping that recurs. Halfway down the hill is the Rill and Cold Bath, originally the Cave of Proserpina, daughter of Ceres, who is to be encountered shortly. Further down, at the

Left: *Queen Caroline monument by Michael Rysbrack; Stowe, Buckinghamshire.*

Below: *The British Worthies by Michael Rysbrack and Peter Scheemakers; Stowe, Buckinghamshire.*

entrance to the Lime Walk, stands Antinous, after the original in the Belvedere Court. This figure was often confused with Apollo at the time and is usually referred to as such. In his role as one of the gods of Arcadia, Apollo would fit into the nature theme of these lower parts of the garden.

Out at the other end of the Lime Walk, Venus's Vale comes as a surprise. A sloping valley bears two cascades and a general design in triangular form. Above the upper cascade is a lead Medici Venus forming a triangle with two attendant amorini on swans (though the amorini have now disappeared), with the presiding goddess of the vale at the highest vantage point. Venus has an association with gardens as a goddess of fecundity. Extending the triangle out into the vale, two rustic figures are seen, Pan and Faun, two of Van Nost's best productions. They look out to the countryside beyond, as if actors on a stage. Love and the countryside are therefore the themes of this area, as compared with the martial activity up above.

Further on in the circuit, Bridgeman's vestigial amphitheatre provides a clearing in which another triangle of figures is grouped. Mercury, at the apex, and Ceres and Bacchus continue the earlier theme of nature's bounty. Mercury, messenger of the gods, is a sort of 'link man' in this process.

The owner of the gardens at this time was General James Dormer, who had served with the Duke of Marlborough, and thus the contrast between a military career and a country retreat links his own life with the programme of the gardens. As both sculptures by Scheemakers had associations of death, there may be also a connection (in Dormer's thoughts) with his terminal illness in 1741. There are, or were, a number of statues in niches round the exterior of the house – Apollo, Venus, a Dancing Faun, Ceres, a Bacchanal – which foreshadow the sculpture in the garden. Another vanished piece is the Hercules and Antaeus in the central niche in the Pyramid, which might have echoed Dormer's own triumph over the French in earlier days.

At Stourhead, Wiltshire, there is no consistent or worked-out programme of sculpture, but individual pieces may contribute to the meaning or interpretation of the garden. The Hercules by Rysbrack (based on the Farnese original but modelled on the limbs of London boxers) in the centre of the Pantheon may indicate the theme of the Choice of Hercules, standard in Renaissance iconography, between the steep path to Virtue and the easy, pleasant path to Vice, if one accepts that along the Stourhead circuit there is just such a choice between the zigzag path up to the Temple of Apollo and a gentle descent back to the Palladian bridge (and that the

River God by John Cheere; Stourhead, Wiltshire.

garden holds such a meaning). The River God in white lead by John Cheere in the grotto has been shown to be a copy of the River God of Tiber who points the way to Aeneas to found Rome: Stourhead is thus seen as a fount and source of a new civilisation parallel to Rome.

But the most elaborate programme of all was at Stowe, Buckinghamshire. This, the most celebrated garden of its day, was overtly political in its message. At the time there were over two hundred pieces of sculpture, but many were sold off in a number of sales, principally in 1848 and 1921. However, there are plentiful descriptions, so we know what was there originally, and the surviving items are being supplemented by copies of the originals which are located elsewhere or, in some cases, by the return of the originals. From the sculpture alone it would be possible to chart the course of the owner's politics even if we knew nothing about him from other sources.

Sir Richard Temple (1675-1749) inherited Stowe in 1697. He was a Whig who fell out of favour during the period of Tory dominance in the reign of Queen Anne and lost his army commands. The accession of George I in 1714 turned the tide in his fortunes, and he regained his high position in the army and was created Viscount Cobham in 1718. Although the usual approach to the gardens, and thence to the house, was at that time from the south, the entrance court on the north front of the house was imposingly graced by a magnificent equestrian statue, in lead, of George I by

Van Nost the Younger. This was originally further away from the house than it is now. The king is depicted as a Roman emperor on his horse (the inscription relates him to Caesar), thereby simultaneously giving George a classical dignity and attributes and paying a tribute to ancient Rome as a source of inspiration and civilisation.

For a time Lord Cobham kept in with the king and the government under the Whig Sir Robert Walpole. Two other statues testify to this period in Cobham's life and career. One is the monument (*c.*1725) to Princess (later Queen) Caroline, wife of George II, who succeeded in 1727. It consists of a statue of Caroline in stone on a base of four tall columns, attributed to Rysbrack. The other was the (lost) statue of George II himself on top of a Corinthian column. However, during the 1730s Lord Cobham's political interests turned in another direction. After Walpole's Excise Bill of 1733, Cobham became the centre of a group of disaffected Whigs who formed an opposition to the Whig administration. This group sought a return to an earlier form of liberty and incorrupt service claimed to have been demonstrated in Britain from the time of King Alfred to that of William III but then supposedly lost. This change is reflected markedly in the garden works, both sculpture and buildings.

William Kent's Temple of Ancient Virtue, in the area known as the Elysian Fields, was juxtaposed with the Temple of Modern Virtue, a ruin consisting of little more than a wall and rubble. The contrast was sharp and effective and the satire was not lost on visitors. The Temple of Ancient Virtue housed four figures epitomising their respective qualities and achievements: Lycurgus as the wisest law-giver; Socrates as the greatest philosopher; Homer as the finest poet; and Epaminondas as the most illustrious commander. George Bickham's guidebook *The Beauties of Stow* [sic] pointedly identifies them with Whig Opposition ideology: they aimed 'to establish a well-regulated Constitution, to

Homer by Peter Scheemakers; Cottesbrooke Hall, Northamptonshire (originally in the Temple of Ancient Virtue at Stowe).

dictate the soundest Morality, to place Virtue in the most amiable Light, and bravely to defend a People's Liberty'. To press the point home, a headless statue beside the crumbling Temple of Modern Virtue could be recognised from its robes as Walpole, head of the government in power.

In the Elysian Fields, too, stands William Kent's curving gallery of British Worthies, busts of sixteen Britons (half of them sculpted by Rysbrack, the rest by Scheemakers) who embodied the qualities of the Temple of Ancient Virtue which faces them across the river. Half represented action while the remainder were great thinkers. This Temple of the Worthies replaced an earlier temple (elsewhere in the grounds) built by Gibbs to house eight of the busts. It is a strongly political statement, important almost as much for who was left out (for example, there are no churchmen, the Anglican church being regarded as Tory by Lord Cobham and his allies) as for who was portrayed. The busts include those of Gresham (builder of the Royal Exchange), Inigo Jones, Milton, Shakespeare, Locke, Bacon, King Alfred (whom they supposed to be founder of the British constitution and of many aspects of British civilisation), Drake, Raleigh, Queen Elizabeth I and William III, who 'by bold and generous Enterprize, preserved the Liberty and Religion of *Great Britain*'. As counterpoint to this impressive assembly an inscription on the rear of the building pays tribute to the memory of an Italian, one Signor Fido, whose virtues are recited before the revelation that he was not a man but a greyhound.

The centrepiece of the gallery is surmounted by a pyramid with a head of Mercury (now lost) in a niche. This relates the Temple to the Elysian Fields round it, for Mercury conducted the souls of heroes to the Fields.

The political bias of the garden artefacts is also discernible in the Temple of Friendship and the Gothic Temple. The former, now a shell after a disastrous fire, originally contained ten pedestals with the busts of Cobham and his friends and associates, including William Pitt the Elder, Richard Grenville, George Lyttelton and the Prince of Wales, sculpted by Scheemakers and Thomas Adye. These were not just friends, but political friends, those who became known as the 'Cobham Cubs' or the 'Boy Patriots', the Whig Opposition circle. As time passed, so squabbles among the friends led to removal of some of the busts.

The Gothic Temple stood as a symbol of defiance to the establishment, promoting native virtues against 'Roman decadence', the excesses of late classical Rome, to which Walpole's government was compared. This temple was formerly known as the Temple of

Liberty, and round it stood Rysbrack's statues of the Saxon deities who gave their names to the days of the week. The deities had originally surrounded an altar on open ground at Stowe called the Saxon Temple. Gothic and Saxon thus converge in the name of liberty – the two were seen as part of the same native tradition (Gothic being taken to be an English style of architecture).

Other sculptures included a tribute to Cobham himself, erected by Lady Cobham in 1747 in honour of her husband, and the Grenville column which commemorates Thomas Grenville, a nephew who perished in a naval battle. On top is a statue not of Grenville but of Heroic Poetry. This was moved from the Grecian Valley to its present position facing the British Worthies, which gives it an association with them. Another sculpture is at once tribute and satire, and that is Congreve's Monument by Kent (1736) on an island in the lake. A squatting monkey surveys himself in a mirror, with an inscription to the effect that comedy is the imitation of life and the mirror of fashion. An epitaph bestows praise on the wit and manners of the great comic dramatist.

Other themes run through the garden sculpture and buildings, notably Love and Action. Erotic love was celebrated in the grotto which contained a marble statue of Venus on a pedestal; the flanking shell temples each contained a pair of embracing amorini on pedestals; a gilt copy of the Medici Venus featured in the centre of Vanbrugh's Rotunda; and other buildings such as the Temple of Venus and Dido's Cave expressed the same theme, in painted rather than sculptural form. All the paintings have disappeared, however. Action was embodied in sculpture and decoration on the Temple of Concord and Victory and the Palladian Bridge, while individual figures in prominent positions included Hercules and Antaeus (attributed to Carpenter) and a Gladiator. Action is, of course, a theme also found in the British Worthies.

Rococo and after

Although rococo did not become established generally in the arts in Britain until 1730 or so, tendencies towards it in sculpture can be detected in some of Van Nost's and Carpenter's work, when we consider that some of their figures appear later in truly rococo form as porcelain miniatures. Such figures as the shepherd-piper or the haymaker and gardener depicted at Wrest Park early in the eighteenth century point the way forward to the naturalistic, charming or amusing figures to be encountered in later years. A key date in the development of garden sculpture is 1737, the year in which Carpenter died and John Cheere (1709-87) took over the Van Nost yard. Cheere is the master of rococo garden sculpture, yet much of his work is still classical, and he continued to use the Van Nost moulds or models. He was the younger brother of the greater sculptor Sir Henry Cheere, for whom he worked for a while.

J. T. Smith, in his book *The Streets of London*, is scathing about the quality of the work of Cheere and others, but at least he has left us a useful description of Cheere's yard: 'The figures were cast in lead as large as life, and frequently painted with an intention to resemble nature. They consisted of Punch, Harlequin, Columbine, and other pantomimical characters, mowers whetting their scythes; hay-makers resting on their rakes; game-keepers in the act of shooting, and *Roman* soldiers with *firelocks*; but, above all, that of an African kneeling with a sun-dial upon his head found the most extensive sale.' It will be noticed that this list is a mixture of figures already encountered and the new elements of *commedia dell'arte* and the gamekeeper shooting, a realistic version of which survives in full colour at Biel, Lothian.

Cheere produced an enormous number of figures in both lead and plaster and took over a further two yards in the Hyde Park district. His major commissions included Castle Hill (Devon), Chiswick, Stourhead, Castle Howard, Kedleston Hall (Derbyshire), Copped Hall (Essex), Bowood (Wiltshire) and Blair Castle (Tayside). Many other commissions are attributed to him with a degree of certainty, including Painshill, Wilton and Wrest Park. The largest commission of all was to produce ninety-eight lead pieces for the royal palace of Queluz, near Lisbon, in 1756. Sometimes lead copies would be made of stone sculpture already *in situ*, as in the case of the Portland stone seats, lions and sphinxes at Chiswick, all of which Cheere reproduced for Lord Burlington, so that matching stone and lead pieces stood side by side. At Castle Howard he produced a Dancing Faun and a Roman Gladiator for Lord Carlisle to complement Carpenter's earlier work. He reworked Van Nost's kneeling Blackamoor for Okeover Hall, Staffordshire, in 1741 and two years later altered it again to Father Time (still kneeling and supporting a sundial) at Blair Castle.

At Blair there was a duplicate of Cheere's gamekeeper at Biel but this has now gone. At Wrest Park four groups purchased by the second Earl de Grey in the 1830s are attributed to Cheere: Venus and Adonis, Aeneas and Anchises, Diana and Endymion and the Abduction of Helen. These groups attest to Cheere's skill as a sculptor, creating figures which might be based on earlier originals but which exhibit high standards of the lead-caster's art.

At Stourhead Cheere's most striking contribution is the River God in white lead (1751), but he also produced the Sleeping Nymph in the grotto and eight statues for the niches in the Temple of Apollo on top of the hill – Pomona, Minerva, Urania, Venus, a Vestal, Mercury, Apollo and Bacchus. The lead Bacchus and Venus in the niches of the Pantheon may be two of these figures which have long since left their former abode.

Cheere's commissions for the second Duke of Atholl at Blair centred round a designated Hercules garden, which included a Hercules Walk (past Cheere's statue of the Farnese Hercules, 1743),

Calydonian Boar by Peter Scheemakers; Chatsworth, Derbyshire.

a Hercules Park and a Hercules Wilderness. This whole area, a considerable site of more than 3.5 hectares, was walled in and adorned with Chinese railings and many sculptures. Christopher Dingwall has given an account of the figures that followed Hercules from Cheere's workshop: the Four Seasons in marble, the Father Time mentioned above and twenty lead pieces of assorted rococo. These covered the range of Cheere's output: first came the classical figures, Mercury, Bacchus and Pomona. Then there were contemporary representations: a pair of haymakers, a pair of gardeners, a sailor and his girl dancing, a girl in Highland dress, a piper, a fiddler, a pair of Dutch skaters and the life-size gamekeeper as at Biel. Finally, a *commedia dell'arte* group comprised male and female Harlequins, Columbine, Pierrot and Scaramouch. There was no sculpture programme as such, but the effect would have been a miniature Versailles in rococo, the seriousness of Louis's purpose reduced to whimsy and entertainment, but all in the name of the moral hero Hercules (that is, the owner).

Other sculptors of the period who made their mark in garden works were Roubiliac, Rysbrack and Scheemakers, all of whom worked in stone. Louis François Roubiliac (1702/5-62) made hardly any garden sculpture but was known for two pieces composed for Jonathan Tyers at Vauxhall Gardens, London: a Milton in lead and a marble statue of Handel (1738), a commission he received on Cheere's recommendation, which is now in the Victoria and Albert Museum. The informal (not to say casual – one slipper is off the foot) and naturalistic pose is often taken to be a sign of the new rococo approach to sculpture. Handel is depicted playing a lyre, and there are overtones of either Apollo or Orpheus (interpretations have varied) but the casual pose undermines and deflates the sense of reverence that would normally accompany those classical beings. It was a fine piece of sculpture for Vauxhall and also a tribute to the composer, whose music was heard not only there but at the other pleasure gardens, such as Marylebone.

Michael Rysbrack (1694-1770), a native of Antwerp, came to England about 1720 and rapidly became the leading sculptor in the land, working in marble (often from a terracotta model) to produce a considerable number of high-quality busts of both historical and contemporary figures. We have already encountered his British Worthies and Saxon Deities at Stowe; he also made Hercules and Flora for Henry Hoare at Stourhead. A rival was Peter Scheemakers (1691-1781), also of Antwerp and also in England by about 1720. Like Rysbrack, his style was baroque/classical rather than rococo, and they sometimes even essayed the same figure (such as the

Gardener; Burton Agnes, East Yorkshire.

Mower; Bicton, Devon.

equestrian William III), though Rysbrack is usually judged to be the greater of the two. Scheemakers completed the second set of British Worthies at Stowe and the four statues in the Temple of Ancient Virtue, and both men sculpted funerary monuments. Scheemakers' figures of the Lion Attacking the Horse and the Dying Gladiator at Rousham have been mentioned earlier, and he also carved some of the vases in Carrara marble now to be found at Anglesey Abbey, Cambridgeshire. The Calydonian Boar and Wolf commissioned *c.*1740 for Chiswick and attributed to Scheemakers are now to be found in the forecourt at Chatsworth.

Although we have been concerned with the major creators of sculpture, many pieces were produced by statuaries of whom little is known. One such was Benjamin Rackstrow, who advertised that he would make or mend lead figures for gardens and fountains.

There are several delightful collections of sculpture of this period, though individual items are not always easy to date. Bicton Park, Devon, has some small modern reproductions, but of prime sculptural interest is the so-called Four Seasons at the corners of the main pond. Even though they do not have much to do with the seasons, they form an intriguing quartet. One is a mower sharpening his scythe, unfortunately in poor repair. This figure proves the point about difficulty of dating and attribution: it was known early in the eighteenth century yet was still being produced by Cheere up to fifty years later. Another is the figure known sometimes as a shepherdess, sometimes as an orange-seller, though at Bicton the fruit has disappeared from her raised left hand. This figure appears in many gardens. Another is indisputably a shepherdess with a crook in her left hand and a lamb cradled in her right arm. The fourth is a man wearing a hat and in contemporary costume (as they all are). In the 'Seasons' interpretation he would presumably have to be Winter but has no appropriate attributes.

In a private garden near York there is a superlative assembly of lead figures restored in off-white paint to resemble stone. One or two can be dated to the 1720s or 1730s; others may be later. They are, in any event, the essence of rococo. Among them are a Roman soldier, a piper with one leg crossed (the traditional figure but with some details clearly modelled separately), Fame with her trumpet, the orange-seller, a female with a spear, a décolleté female in contemporary dress, and a tipsy sailor with a small barrel in one hand and raising a tankard in the other (a figure known as the Buccaneer). This mingling of naturalistic contemporary figures with a few from antique times is characteristic of Cheere's output.

Wallington, Northumberland, has a walled garden with a long terrace. Along the wall bordering the terrace are a number of small lead figures which may originally have come from an artificial mound in front of two ponds elsewhere on the estate or from the family's house in Newcastle. Several are in the manner of Cheere and may well have been one of his commissions, similar to the collection ordered for Blair Castle. A Neptune with trident stands on top of the gateway, while Perseus, Venus, Mars and Flora accompany a country girl holding a sheaf of flowers, a Dutch sea captain in a cap smoking a long pipe, and a cheerful figure known as 'Singing Simon' with one arm raised, all in contemporary costume. As with the previous assemblage, the collection is decidedly Cheerean in its mixture.

'Singing Simon'; Wallington, Northumberland.

Left: *Orange-seller; private collection.*

Below: *Lion attributed to John Cheere; Anglesey Abbey, Cambridgeshire.*

Left: *Flora (Farnese) by John Cheere; Southill, Bedfordshire.*

Right: *Girl with bird's nest; Burton Agnes, East Yorkshire.*

In many instances a collection has been assembled from one or more sources long after the original commissions, so that statues may be seen today in settings far from those intended. In the case of Southill, Bedfordshire, several of Cheere's leads were purchased by Samuel Whitbread in 1812, and the collection survives. It includes Samson slaying a Philistine, the Rape of Proserpina, Minerva, the Farnese Flora and a pair of Sleeping Nymphs. Although it is a fine assembly, it represents only the classical side of Cheere's output, without the contemporary figures.

Another collection, much larger and embracing sculpture from many sources and from many different periods, is to be seen at Anglesey Abbey, Cambridgeshire. The first Lord Fairhaven laid out the gardens from 1930 and collected widely to adorn and point up the layout, especially its formal lines. Many items come from the continent, including twelve busts of Roman emperors in marble (Italian, early eighteenth-century) and elaborate bronze satyr and harpy urns from Bagatelle, France (nineteenth-century).

But pride of place goes to the eighteenth-century English works. Particularly noteworthy are Van Nost's Samson and the Philistine, Rysbrack's Tiw (from his Saxon Deities formerly at Stowe, as previously described), two vases in Carrara marble by Scheemakers and two by Laurent Delvaux, two satyr herms in chalk, an Apollo and a Diana *c.*1720, two lead sphinxes and a Diana and Endymion attributed to Cheere, a lion and lioness, two lead figures of 'Painting' and 'Sculpture' and two of Roman women (all from the Temple of Victory at Stowe), and a shepherdess with a lamb and Minerva in armour, both from the tradition of Van Nost, Carpenter and Cheere.

The great number of classical figures found in the eighteenth century caused some critical comment from people such as John Wesley, who deplored 'heathen deities', and the author of *The Connoisseur* in 1756, who was concerned that more attention was given to Pan and his like than to Christian representations.

Rococo statuary attracted some ridicule, though often the satire was directed at the owners. Robert Lloyd's *The Cit's Country Box* (1757) mocks Sir Thrifty, the city-dweller who has purchased a small estate in the country. Within its confines he tries to pack all the features that would normally be found in a large-scale landscape park. Sculpture is part of the crowded scene:

> 'And now from Hyde-Park Corner come
> The Gods of Athens, and of Rome.
> Here squabby Cupids take their places,
> With Venus, and the clumsy Graces:
> Apollo there, with aim so clever
> Stretches his leaden bow for ever;
> And there, without the power to fly,
> Stands fix'd a tip-toe Mercury.'

In similar vein David Garrick in *The Clandestine Marriage* (1765) has Lord Ogleby look over the garden of the *nouveau riche* Mr Sterling: 'Wonderful improvements! the four seasons in lead, the flying Mercury, and the basin with Neptune in the Middle, are all in the very extreme of fine taste. You have as many rich figures as the man at Hyde-Park Corner' (Cheere, of course). A few years later, Richard Cumberland imagined a visit to Sir Theodore and Lady Thimble (1785), where he came across what he thought was his host in an attitude of great politeness, 'but, how was I surprised to find, in place of Sir Theodore, a leaden statue on a pair of scates, painted in a blue and gold coat, with a red waistcoat.'

In 1789 John Moore's *Zaluco* was published, which contains some mockery at the expense of a Mr Transfer who had retired from London and set up in the country 'with no other company than a few gods and goddesses which he had bought in Piccadilly, and placed in his garden'. He has great trouble in distinguishing between them: 'that there statue I take to be – let me recollect – yes, I take that to be either Venus or Vulcan, but upon my word I cannot exactly tell which', whereupon the gardener has to help him out.

The Abduction of Helen, attributed to John Cheere; Wrest Park, Bedfordshire.

The visitor replies drily that it is indeed a problem since they are both made of the same material. Transfer claims that he took a long time to grasp their names 'but I know them all pretty well now – That there man, in the highland garb is Mars. And the name of the old fellow with the pitchfork is Neptune.'

The Grand Tour had considerable implications for garden sculpture in the eighteenth century. Not only did the well-born young go and see for themselves the marvels of classical ruins and Renaissance gardens thick with sculpture that inspired them to create something similar at home, but they often brought back with them antique relics with which to adorn their gardens. Lord Burlington, for example, brought three figures from Hadrian's Villa at Tivoli to put in his exedra at Chiswick. These were later claimed to represent Caesar, Pompey and Cicero, though this is doubtful, and in any case the heads do not necessarily belong to the bodies to which they have been attached. Such was the appetite for classical sculpture that 'restoration' was big business in Italy and some none too scrupulous practices flourished. Some extremely misguided and botched repair jobs were carried out, the results of which can be seen, for instance, in some of the Townley Collection in the British Museum.

Above: *Tiw by Michael Rysbrack; Anglesey Abbey, Cambridgeshire (originally at Stowe).*

Right: *Drummer boy attributed to John Cheere; private collection.*

Another who returned well-laden from the Grand Tour was Charles Hamilton of Painshill. His prize was a figure, 2.5 metres high, of Bacchus, a Greek original found in Rome, but he had also some smaller pieces and a set of busts of twelve of the Roman emperors, while the Tower contained a Minerva and Flora and the Mausoleum some busts and funerary relics.

It has been mentioned that the development of Coade stone from *c*.1770 spelled the end for leadwork. This artificial stone, resembling limestone, was a ceramic capable of being formed into attractive and hard-wearing pieces that could be finely modelled and the moulds reused to produce copies. Vases and pedestals were soon in production; the 1784 catalogue lists forty-seven different vase designs, though many are variations on basic shapes. Coade could imitate leadwork, for example the pair of lions produced for Audley End, Essex, in 1786. More animals, including elephants and Indian bulls, were commissioned by Sir Charles Cockerell for his Indian-influenced estate of Sezincote, Gloucestershire. Memorials and sundials were popular productions, and fountains, such as the Triton fountain at Petworth, West Sussex, after Giambologna, gave great scope. People were sculpted too; George III as a Roman emperor stands at Taplow Court, Buckinghamshire (1804), and the classical deities (Ceres, Flora, Pomona and others) followed the familiar eighteenth-century tradition. There were several sphinxes, a large pair of which are at Croome Court, Worcestershire (1795), although they are Grecian rather than Egyptian. However, there are two upright Egyptian figures at Buscot Park, Oxfordshire (1800), after Hadrian's statue of his favourite Antinous as a Pharaoh. Ancient Britain was

Antinous as a Pharaoh in Coade stone; Buscot Park, Oxfordshire.

also represented: a Druid is to be found at Croome Court and another, now in ruinous condition, at Shugborough, Staffordshire, was perched on Thomas Wright's classical ruins at a later date.

A particularly splendid Coade work is the River God at Ham House, Surrey, which was the first item in the 1784 catalogue. This was not a fountain figure but a set piece with the rock and the water gushing from his urn all in Coade stone, although the composition is itself set on a real rock. There appears to have been much hand-modelling of the features of the face in particular, carried out after the figure had come out of the moulds but before it had set hard and been fired in the kiln.

Right: *Satyr term in chalk; Anglesey Abbey, Cambridgeshire.*

Below: *River God in Coade stone; Ham House, Surrey.*

The nineteenth century

Until well into the nineteenth century Coade stone and similar forms of artificial stone produced by other firms made the running alongside cast iron and other metals such as spelter (see pages 8-11). However, wealthy clients might commission individual works in marble or else import them, as Baron Ferdinand de Rothschild did to such spectacular effect at Waddesdon Manor, Buckinghamshire.

There are several examples of the so-called 'High Victorian' style of garden, which brought back the fashion for Italianate design. Although there was an Italian garden at Mount Edgcumbe, Cornwall, in the very early years of the century, many designers were influenced by the versatile architect Sir Charles Barry, who employed Italian Renaissance features such as terracing, balustrades, steps, formal paths, urns, pools and fountains. From about 1840 such features found their way into many gardens laid out in geometrical patterns. However, the emphasis on sculpture in Italian gardens was not reflected in this Victorian revival in Britain. Some of the gardens that have survived, like Barry's extravagant stepped terraces at Shrubland, Suffolk, or the terrace gardens at Bowood, have little sculpture, though where there were fountains sculptural groups often appeared. Barry's designs for Trentham, Staffordshire, included a number of figures, as did Sir Richard Westmacott's early work at Wilton, in the Italian parterre garden (1820-1), but the interest was still not as heavily sculptural as in many an Italian garden and was diffused among urns and fountains as well as statues.

In W. A. Nesfield's great parterre garden at Castle Howard (previously and subsequently laid out to lawn) the centrepiece was John Thomas's Atlas fountain in Portland stone (completed 1853). This powerful group consists of Atlas crouching on one knee under the globe, with four Tritons blowing conch shells on the outside of the basin. The top of the globe and each of the conches provided the principal jets of water.

At Grimston, North Yorkshire, Nesfield laid out a path flanked by busts of the twelve Caesars (now gone), called the Emperor's Walk. A similar arrangement was made in the 1870s at Madresfield Court, Worcestershire, where the emperors are set in niches in a long yew hedge. At Alton Towers, Staffordshire, there was much statuary, including the figures that survive along the top of an arcade. Sometimes existing collections of sculpture were added to: thus the sixth Duke of Devonshire, inheriting sculpture by Van Nost, Osgood, Carpenter and Cibber at Chatsworth, commissioned

Above: *Fountain of Love by Waldo Story; Cliveden, Buckinghamshire.*

Opposite page: *Sculpture at Waddesdon Manor, Buckinghamshire: (top) the Pluto and Proserpina fountain by Mozani; (bottom left) Asia by Cassetti; (bottom right) Hercules destroying the Nemean lion by Baratta.*

Wounded Amazon by Francesco Bienaimé; Chatsworth, Derbyshire.

Francesco Bienaimé *c.*1830 to produce a number of classical and neo-classical figures from Carrara marble. Some are the familiar figures of the Apollo Belvedere, the Farnese Hercules and the 'Louvre' Diana, which are now in the Private Gardens, but in addition there were copies of works by contemporary or recent sculptors such as Canova. Sometimes an English sculptor would go to Italy to work, as William Theed the Younger did when he created the figure of Narcissus from Carrara marble in Rome in 1848, a figure which now stands at Anglesey Abbey.

Prince Albert's Italianate gardens at Osborne, Isle of Wight (1847-53), contain a number of works after Italian originals that took advantage of advances in technology. There are two large Medici lions in artificial stone by Austin & Seeley and a bronzed-zinc boy-and-swan fountain, while a bronze Andromeda by the Coalbrookdale Company graces a more elaborate fountain surrounded by eight sea monsters by Theed. Many statues, including the Four Seasons in bronze-coated zinc, adorn the various terrace levels. Austin & Seeley provided the cement pieces while Geiss of Berlin and Miroy Frères of Paris furnished those in zinc.

When the Crystal Palace was moved from Hyde Park to Sydenham, Surrey, after the Great Exhibition, prehistoric monsters in concrete were created to roam on the lake and islands at the eastern end of the central axis of the park (completed 1854) laid out by Joseph Paxton and Edward Milner. This development can be seen in the light of the public interest in natural history which resulted in the founding of the Natural History Museum (model dinosaurs had been seen for the first time at the Crystal Palace).

The Victorian era was a time for proliferation of garden ornament generally, in the form of urns, containers and seats as well as sculpted figures. Cast iron, artificial stone and ceramics were used to produce pieces that were sometimes very elaborate, such as the Lion tazza, a large shallow bowl supported on a central stem and four lions, in Regent's Park, London. The whole was constructed in composition stone by Austin & Seeley.

Fountains played an important part in nineteenth-century gardens. Some have already been mentioned, but in addition fountains with groups can be seen on the grand terrace at Kinmel Park, Clwyd, and at Ascott, Buckinghamshire, while a rockwork fountain from 1861 survives at Erddig, Clwyd. At Ascott, the American sculptor Thomas Waldo Story created for Leopold de Rothschild the Venus fountain with the goddess flanked by horses and also, in what is now the Dutch Garden (a formal area with flower beds), a tall shelved fountain topped by a figure, all in bronze. Château Impney, Droitwich, Worcestershire, has a cast-iron fountain from the Britannia Iron Works with putti astride dolphins blowing water from conches.

The greatest Victorian sculpture garden is undeniably Waddesdon Manor. The site was purchased by Baron Ferdinand de Rothschild in 1874, and on it he built the stupendous château-style mansion and surrounded it with a mixture of formal gardens and undulating slopes and lawn and woodland areas. From Italy and Holland he obtained a large number of figures, most of which are eighteenth-century in origin, some from villas or palaces which were being sold off or closed down. Giuliano Mazani's two early eighteenth-century fountain groups from Colorno near Parma can be seen, one forming the North Fountain on that side of the house, linked to it by a grand drive: the group comprises Triton and the Nereids. The other is the superb Pluto and Proserpina group in the parterre on the south side, a dramatic representation of the abduction, ringed round by other figures.

Among other early eighteenth-century figures in marble – individual pieces on pedestals – are the four Continents by Giacomo Cassetti, each with the attributes deemed appropriate at the time: Europe has a miniature temple to denote civilisation as well as architecture, while the others are conceived in rather more primitive terms. Inside the decorative cast-iron Aviary there is a sculptural group of Minerva and Tritons set on rocks in an alcove, while outside on the Aviary lawn the infant Bacchus plays with a ram (a Florentine work). Some fine copies of classical originals may be singled out, such as Ceres and the Apollo Belvedere, while, instead of the usual Hercules resting after destroying the Nemean lion (the Farnese Hercules), we find him in the act of killing the lion by tearing its jaws apart, a vivid and violent image.

At the end of the century there were manifestations of *fin de siècle* eroticism. The sculptor Waldo Story created for his compatriot William Waldorf Astor, the new owner of Cliveden, a marble Fountain of Love, where three female figures, attended by cupids, are grouped around a huge shell in a state of abandoned intoxication from the effects of the fountain. In similar vein there was an extraordinary array of larger-than-life female figures imported from Italy, originally intended for Whitley Court in Surrey, which were purchased by Ratan Tata, an Indian merchant prince, in 1906 and displayed in the sunken gardens he created in the riverside area adjoining York House, Twickenham, Middlesex. He had a fountain constructed with rocks piled up in the manner of an Italian water theatre, with a Venus accompanied by two horses at the top. Lower down naked figures disport themselves on the rocks in a variety of

Tableau of Nymphs; York House, Twickenham, Middlesex.

Above left: *Nymph by Lucchesi; Chirk Castle, Clwyd.*
Above right: *Faun, Neapolitan; Anglesey Abbey, Cambridgeshire.*

uninhibited poses, sprawling, climbing, pleading or offering.

Less flamboyant but partly for titillatory effect are the four nymphs in bronze by Andrea Lucchesi (1860-1925) at Chirk Castle, Clwyd, two of which mark the entrance to the upper lawn, while a third watches over a pool which was not, however, formed until after the Second World War.

The twentieth century

Sculpture did not play a large part in the garden movements of the late nineteenth and early twentieth centuries. In the wild woodland gardens of William Robinson, the Arts and Crafts gardens or those created by the Jekyll and Lutyens partnership, fountains might sometimes be found but not much in the way of statuary. Such sculpture as there was is to be seen in the Italianate gardens which followed on in the wake of the High Victorian revival of interest in Italian forms. William Waldorf Astor, first Viscount Astor, imported a great deal of Italian sculpture, first to Cliveden from 1893 and then to Hever Castle, Kent, which he bought in 1903 and moved to in 1906. At Cliveden he created the Long Garden, furnished it with the eighteenth-century sculpture described earlier and also erected on the south side of the house the balustrade which had come from the Villa Borghese. It was decorated with two seventeenth-century French hunting figures. Roman sarcophagi, urns and various other statues at Cliveden testify to his great love of Italy.

It was at Hever, though, that Astor created the great Italian Garden, which contains a superb collection of classical and Renaissance sculpture. He collected a great deal when he was American minister in Italy and brought it to Hever from 1903 to 1908. The Italian Garden covers nearly 2 hectares, flanked along one side for over 200 metres by the Pompeian Wall, which is divided into bays to display fragments of stonework, statues, vases and sarcophagi placed in no particular scheme or pattern but surrounded by flowers and shrubs to provide a setting. There is a series of bay grottoes, classical colonnades, a loggia and a piazza leading on to the lake.

An Englishman with a similar fondness for Italy was Sir George Sitwell, who began work on the grounds of his family seat of Renishaw Hall, Derbyshire, in 1887. During the 1890s he studied Italian gardens and wrote a book in 1909 on the principles to be derived from them. At Renishaw he attempted to blend the garden with the general landscape and to create a feeling of wonder and a scene that would appeal to the imagination and all the senses. The sense of Italy was conveyed particularly in the statuary and water. Figures of Diana and Neptune, ascribed to Caligari, are centrally placed along the main axis, while the so-called giants, oversize figures of Samson and Hercules, stand sentinel at its southern boundary. Both pairs of figures stand on the side of descending steps and look outwards, away from the house, as if to direct the visitor towards the park and the landscape beyond. Meanwhile, between the woods and the garden, stand another pair, Achilles and Minerva (though generally called 'Warrior' and 'Amazon'), also marking the transition from one part to another. Other works, such as the winged gilt statue of Fame, stand solo to one side. Fame was by the Victorian sculptor Thomas Thornycroft and originally crowned a group forming the 'Poets' fountain' in Park Lane, London.

Another Englishman well-known for being influenced by Italy was Harold Peto (1854-1933). An architect and landscape gardener, he was responsible for a large number of commissions in Britain and abroad, but with regard to sculpture his work at his own home of Iford Manor, Wiltshire, and at Buscot Park is of greatest moment. He worked on Iford from 1898 till his death, building the terraced garden on a fairly steep slope on which he harmonised plants with architecture. Relics and fragments, such as columns or colonnades, sarcophagi, friezes, reliefs, well-heads and sculptures of people and animals, date from classical times onwards, through Byzantine to the Renaissance. These are supplemented by one or two contemporary pieces such as the cast taken from the original in Rome of Romulus and Remus with the wolf, or the column dedicated to Edward VII raised in the First World War. The Cloisters, in particular, contain many venerable fragments, some of which are incorporated in the fabric of the building.

Peto's water garden at Buscot Park consists of a long vista along which passes a strip of water through a changing series of narrow channels, circular and square basins (one with the Boy and Dolphin fountain), under a small balustraded bridge and between yew hedges which shield a number of figures including classical terms and a playful set of four children dressed up, one as a Roman soldier with a mongoose perched on his helmet. The statuary elsewhere in the gardens includes the pair of Coade Egyptian figures, mentioned on page 65.

The three prominent names in British garden sculpture of the twentieth century are Henry Moore, Barbara Hepworth and Elisabeth Frink. A great deal of the sculpture of Henry Moore (1898-1986) was intended for outdoors (he claimed that 'sculpture is an art of the open air'), and the positioning of a piece in a landscape setting is vital, taking into account that it will be seen from a number of angles, each with its own background of lawn, trees and so on. Moore's output was prolific, and even when he essayed abstract forms the figurative and expressive tend to break through, and subconscious, sometimes primitive, feelings are conveyed through them, however remote they may appear to be from the

Left: *Samson; Renishaw Hall, Derbyshire.*

Right: *Fame by Thomas Thornycroft; Renishaw Hall, Derbyshire.*

Below: *Pompeian Wall; Italian Garden, Hever Castle, Kent.*

Above: *'War Horse' by Elisabeth Frink; Chatsworth, Derbyshire.*

Below: *'The Girl with Doves' by David Wynne; Easton Grey, Wiltshire.*

representational. Particular locations matter: when a collection of Moore's works was displayed in the Bagatelle Gardens in Paris, some felt that the effect had been diminished by taking them from their originally intended settings. Many were subsequently displayed in Bretton Country Park, South Yorkshire, which suited them much better. In his own garden at Hoglands, Hertfordshire, the pieces are spaced apart so that the eye is led from one to another, sometimes providing a unity of shape, sometimes a contrast. The figures range from a relatively representational female sitting backwards to a more abstract version of the same position, and to pieces that are twisted and convoluted in form yet seem to be limbs or an enormous mouth. Several are paired as if they were man and woman. The overall effect, however distorted the shapes, is of a community of individuals expressing various energies and states of feeling. Moore himself believed there was 'no background to sculpture better than the sky, because you are contrasting solid form with its opposite, space'. He also delighted in the tactile qualities of his materials and encouraged people to touch his work.

Among many locations in which Moore's work can be seen are Dartington Hall, Devon; Scotney Castle, Kent; Hyde Park, London (the arch which is half sculpture, half architecture); Greenwich Park, London; and Glenkiln, Dumfries (where Moore thought his work looked best).

Dame Barbara Hepworth (1903-75) often worked in abstract forms which in many cases express a human feeling, and her creations went through a number of phases. Like Moore, in the 1930s she often explored the relationship between two objects and forms, and after the Second World War she spent time exploring oval shapes. In the 1960s she produced much work in relief. Near the lake in Dulwich Park, south London, is her 'Two Forms: Divided Circle' (1970). Her 'Family of Man' (also 1970) has been displayed at the Yorkshire Sculpture Park, South Yorkshire, where the figures relate to each other and to the earth they grow out of, like trees. In the relatively small area of her own garden in St Ives, Cornwall, her shapes and forms are set against colourful vegetation, again relating the sculpture to nature.

Dame Elisabeth Frink (1930-92) concentrated on the male figure and also on animals, especially horses. One of the best examples is her bronze 'War Horse' (1991) at Chatsworth. Like the figures at Renishaw, it faces away from the house, at the far end of the Canal Pond, where a classical piece ought to be in a formal layout but here creating a very different effect. There may be some irony in the title – it looks rather dumpy – and some ambiguity too ('war horse' meaning veteran, perhaps suggesting the long history of the gardens). Her own head appears nearby, sculpted by Angela Conner (1993) as a tribute. Another horse is at Goodwood, West Sussex (1980), while her 'Running Man' (1978) shows the energy and movement which she said she got from Rodin. Her work was particularly concerned with feelings and the conveying of emotions. Her 'Seated Man II' (1986) in bronze thoughtfully surveys the pond at Hat Hill Copse, West Sussex.

Among the works of other artists, Ben Nicholson's 'White Relief' (1937-8) may be singled out, a slab or panel of white marble 10 by 5 metres, which Sir Geoffrey Jellicoe placed in front of a pool at Sutton Place, Surrey, so that its gradations of plane and relief are reflected in the water.

Sculpture parks have been a phenomenon of post-war times. The idea is to display modern sculpture either in temporary exhibitions or permanently. The parks are usually spacious, which means that large works are more suitable than small ones. The park at Hat Hill, Goodwood, which opened in autumn 1994, is probably the most intricate and includes a high-tech educational gallery with information about the artists. The park is purpose-designed so that individual pieces are shown in isolation in clearings or among trees, or as focal points terminating vistas. Pieces are intended to be displayed for up to three years, and young sculptors are encouraged. Nigel Hall, for example, created 'Soglio', a huge circle with cross pieces in corten steel. Best-known is probably Yorkshire Sculpture Park, near Wakefield, which has an extension, Bretton Country Park, an eighteenth-century park, where sculptures such as Henry Moore's can find an appropriate and effective home in a slightly rough and rugged landscape – a different concept from the designed sculpture park. The Yorkshire Sculpture Park puts on regular exhibitions, for example of the work of Igor Mitoraj in marble and bronze, which includes parts of faces and torsos. Another sculpture park is at Margam, Glamorgan, while there are also displays of sculpture in gardens that are not dedicated sculpture gardens, such as Harlow Car, Harrogate. The Chiltern Sculpture Trail, Oxfordshire, contains over twenty contemporary works related to their woodland setting.

A different sort of sculpture garden is the private and personal one of Ian Hamilton Finlay at Stonypath, Strathclyde. This garden, with its witty references and associations, some of which have a political point, partly echoes the eighteenth-century literary garden of Shenstone at the Leasowes, West Midlands, which had inscriptions and moral lessons. At Stonypath a young birch grove used to bear

Above: *'Place'; Forest of Dean Sculpture Trail, Gloucestershire.*
Below left: *'Knife Edge' by Henry Moore; Greenwich Park, London.*
Below right: *Sabine Rape by Ivor Abrahams after Giambologna; Painshill, Surrey.*

the inscription 'Bring back the birch', while a nuclear submarine periscope pokes up from the grass. An 'aircraft-carrier' table is 'bombed' by hungry birds diving on to it. Broken classical columns hark back to Poussin's paintings, and a slab refers to Claude and Poussin by name. Power and destruction are the main themes, with resonances from many cultures past and present.

Environmental sculptures are to be found in natural woodland settings in Grizedale Forest, Cumbria, and the Forest of Dean, Gloucestershire. The items vary from figurative to abstract but are often made from wood. At Grizedale Andy Goldsworthy's 'Sidewinder' (1984-5) uses several curved and serpentine pine trunks together to form a switchback through the trees. His 'The Wall that Went for a Walk' (1990) is even more serpentine and wilful. There are circus figures, arches, a wild boar in mesh and resin, spiders and some abstract constructions.

Late twentieth-century sculptors use many different materials. Serena de la Hey plaits withies to create figures that have humour and character, such as 'Three Running Figures' set out across a field. Mike Smith uses willow rods twisted together to form figures that are slightly mysterious. At Lord Carrington's house at Bledlow, Buckinghamshire, is work commissioned from young sculptors: three large fruits in Kilkenny limestone by Peter Randall-Page, Welsh slate slabs by Alistair Lambert, a two-part marble piece by Paul Vanstone and Paul Barker's French limestone figures tumbling amusingly head over heels down a slope. The garden of Sir Frederick Gibberd at Marsh Lane, Old Harlow, Essex, contains about seventy sculptures from the 1950s onwards, commissioned from contemporary artists such as John Skelton and Gerda Rubinstein. The sculptures are located with a strong sense of space and are integrated into the design with columns, urns and other artefacts.

Others who have produced outdoor sculpture include Austin Wright, who often works in aluminium, creating abstract shapes that nevertheless relate to real forms, for example 'Frond'. David Wynne has worked in Britain, Europe and the USA, and his appealing small bronze, 'The Girl with Doves', at Easton Grey, Wiltshire, expresses freedom and letting go. This is similar to his joyful group of three children at Tresco Abbey, Isles of Scilly. John Edwards is drawn to working in steel, often painted. See also 'Shout' by Glynn Williams on page 85.

But even in the late twentieth century classical sculpture has not been entirely neglected as an influence. Imaginative reworkings are carried out for example by Mitoraj, or by Ivor Abrahams, whose recreation of the lost Sabine statue is at Painshill.

Identifying statues

These are the most commonly encountered classical statues in gardens, with their attributes and meanings. Latin names are used rather than Greek, as has generally and traditionally been the custom. One or two examples are given under each heading but they are not intended to be a comprehensive list.

Alcibiades, Dog of: Alcibiades, an Athenian politician, had a large, good-looking dog whose chief feature was his tail, but Alcibiades had it cut off to provide a talking point among the Athenians in the hope that it would distract them from making derogatory remarks about his own life and behaviour (Blickling, Chatsworth, Wrest Park).

Amorini, putti: cupids or infant attendants of Cupid or Venus (Melbourne Hall, Wilton).

Andromeda: in Greek legend she was chained to a rock and threatened by a dragon but was released and saved by Perseus (Melbourne Hall).

Antaeus: see **Hercules**.

Antinous: youth beloved of the Emperor Hadrian (Rousham), who had him represented as an Egyptian Pharaoh (Buscot Park).

Apollino: 'little Apollo', depicted as a young man with right arm bent and touching his head (Anglesey Abbey, Burton Agnes, Chatsworth, Southill).

Apollo: god of the sun, poetry and music, and sometimes of the countryside; sometimes depicted with a lyre. The most famous form of representation is the Apollo Belvedere (Chatsworth, Waddesdon Manor).

Ariadne: imprisoned on Crete by the Minotaur and released by Theseus; in gardens found in recumbent form after the original in the Belvedere Court and often interpreted as a 'Sleeping Nymph' (Southill, Stourhead, West Wycombe).

Bacchus: god of wine and drink in general; represented holding a bunch of grapes, sometimes wreathed in vine leaves, often with a cup or beaker; sometimes accompanied by a dog (Anglesey Abbey, Hardwick Hall, Rousham).

Calydonian Boar: wild boar slain by Meleager (Chatsworth, Osborne).

Ceres: goddess of corn, crops, food in general; identifiable by a sheaf of wheat, sometimes a cornucopia (Rousham).

Diana: goddess of chastity, the moon, hunting and motherhood; often represented with a small crescent moon on her head, and with a bow and quiver of arrows; sometimes accompanied by a hound or stag (Anglesey Abbey, Chatsworth).

Dog: see **Alcibiades**.

Faunus, Faun: Roman pastoral god, sometimes identifiable with Pan, sometimes with his followers. Occasionally he has horns, but not the goat legs of Pan, though he does have a tail. One pose is with a kid goat slung over his left shoulder. The Faun in Rosso Antico holds grapes up in his right hand and has been mistaken for Bacchus. A young Faun is depicted with a pipe. Although originally identifying a single figure, the term is also applied generically. (Castle Howard, Chatsworth, Rousham.)

Flora: goddess of flowers and the spring, usually identified by a posy of flowers in her hand (Rousham, Southill).

Gladiator: the Borghese Gladiator, with his left arm stretched forward, was often thought to be a discus thrower (St Paul's Walden Bury), but the arm originally had a shield attached to it (Burton Agnes). The Dying Gladiator is to be seen at Rousham and elsewhere.

Hercules: hero associated with gardens, an embodiment of moral virtue and courage. The commonest pose is standing with his club, and wearing the pelt of the Nemean lion he has killed (the Farnese Hercules: Castle Howard, Chatsworth, Stourhead, St Paul's Walden Bury). Other forms include Hercules destroying the giant Antaeus by lifting him off the ground, his source of strength (St Paul's Walden Bury, Studley Royal); and Hercules killing the monster Hydra with his club (Powis; also Goldney, though Hydra is missing).

Herm: a head on a rectangular or downward tapering pedestal.

Juno: queen of the pantheon, Jupiter's consort, sometimes accompanied by a peacock, representing pride (Belvoir).

Lion: often in pairs, after the Medici originals, paw on pommel (Chatsworth, Kedleston, Osborne); lion attacking a horse (Rousham); lion and lioness (Anglesey Abbey).

Medusa: one of the Gorgons, who turned all who saw them to stone; a terrifying figure with snakes for hair, usually depicted as a head decapitated by Perseus (Melbourne Hall).

Meleager: son of the king of Calydon, Greece, famed for destroying a wild boar sent to terrorise the countryside; represented with the head of the boar beside him (Castle Howard).

Mercury: messenger of the gods, usually with winged petasus (simple bowl-like cap), caduceus (rod with two snakes twisting round it) and winged sandals. His most famous pose is after Giambologna – the model for the 'attitude' position in ballet (Hall Barn, Melbourne Hall).

Minerva: goddess of wisdom, also of battle; usually represented in a helmet and with a spear and shield, which sometimes bears the mask of Medusa (Anglesey Abbey, Renishaw, Southill).

Neptune: god of the sea, normally identified by his crown, shaggy beard, trident; may ride a dolphin (Westbury). In fountain groups sometimes accompanied by Nereids (sea-nymphs) and Triton(s).

Nereid: see **Neptune**.

Pan: god of sheep, shepherds and the countryside; he has pointed ears, horns and goat-legs; he sometimes holds or plays the Pan pipes (Painswick, Rousham).

Perseus: saviour of Andromeda and destroyer of Medusa (Melbourne Hall).

Pluto: king of the underworld, usually represented abducting Proserpina.

Priapus: god of orchards and fertility, recognised by enormous erect phallus, as depicted on Roman coins (Bodnant – but without attribute).

Proserpina: daughter of Ceres, associated with growth of seeds in winter/summer cycle; in sculpture usually represented as being abducted by Pluto, often in a fountain group (Southill, Waddesdon Manor).

Putti: see **Amorini**.

Sabine: a group of three, after Giambologna: the Roman soldier, the Sabine woman being carried away, and her helpless father (Painshill).

Silenus: foster-father of Bacchus, notorious for his drinking; in gardens usually depicted as an old man cradling the infant Bacchus (Anglesey Abbey, Castle Howard, Osborne); this image was at one time identified as Saturn about to eat one of his children.

Spinario: seated youth removing a thorn from his foot (Castle Howard).

Term: see **Herm**.

Triton: son of Neptune, a merman with a fish-tail. In some representations there can be several, a genus rather than a single figure (Chatsworth).

Venus: goddess of love, beauty, fertility; also, by association, of gardens; sometimes accompanied by swans and amorini; often depicted in the well-known pose of the Medici Venus (Anglesey Abbey, Chatsworth, Rousham).

Vertumnus: god of orchards and fruit (Anglesey Abbey).

Vulcan: lame blacksmith husband of Venus, recognisable by hammer and anvil (Hampton Court).

Wrestlers: two contending figures based on the original in the Uffizi, Florence (Studley Royal).

In addition there are biblical characters (Cain and Abel or Samson killing a Philistine – often interchangeable: Samson should use the jawbone of an ass as his weapon, while Cain has either a jawbone or a club). There are also personifications of, for example, Envy, Abundance, Justice; the Four Seasons; the Senses; the Continents, often harking back to Ripa (see page 45).

Further reading

Baker, Malcolm. 'Squabby Cupids and Clumsy Graces: Garden Sculpture and Luxury in Eighteenth-Century England', *Oxford Art Journal,* January 1995.

Davis, John. *Antique Garden Ornament.* Antique Collectors' Club, 1991.

Dingwall, Christopher. 'The Hercules Garden at Blair Castle, Perthshire', *Garden History*, 20:2, 1992.

Eyres, Patrick (editor). *New Arcadian Journal*, especially issues which deal with iconography of Rousham (19), Studley Royal (20) and Hercules and Neptune (37/38).

Girard, Jacques. *Versailles Gardens: Sculpture and Mythology.* Sotheby's, 1985.

Haskell, Francis, and Penny, Nicholas. *Taste and the Antique.* Yale University Press, 1981 (subsequently paperback).

Kelly, Alison. 'Coade Stone in Georgian Gardens', *Garden History*, 16:2, 1988.

The Man at Hyde-Park Corner. Catalogue to exhibition of sculpture by John Cheere (1709-87) in Leeds and London, 1974.

Plumptre, George. *Garden Ornament.* Thames & Hudson, 1989.

Strong, Roy. *The Renaissance Garden in England.* Thames & Hudson, 1979 (subsequently paperback).

Whinney, Margaret. *Sculpture in Britain 1530-1830.* Penguin, revised edition 1988.

Below left: *'Two Forms: Divided Circle' by Barbara Hepworth, Dulwich Park, South London.*
Below right: *'Shout' by Glynn Williams; Margam, West Glamorgan.*

Places to visit

Anglesey Abbey, Lode, Cambridgeshire CB5 9EJ (NT). Telephone: 01223 811200.

Belton House, near Grantham, Lincolnshire NG32 2LS (NT). Telephone: 01476 66116.

Belvoir Castle, near Grantham, Lincolnshire NG32 1PD. Telephone: 01476 870262.

Burton Agnes Hall, Burton Agnes, Driffield, East Yorkshire YO25 0ND. Telephone: 01262 490324.

Castle Howard, York YO6 7DA. Telephone: 01653 648333.

Chatsworth, Bakewell, Derbyshire DE45 1PP. Telephone: 01246 582204.

Cliveden, Taplow, Maidenhead, Berkshire SL6 0JA (NT). Telephone: 01628 605069.

Hampton Court Palace, East Molesey, Surrey KT8 9AU. Telephone: 0181-781 9500.

Hever Castle, Edenbridge, Kent TN8 7NG. Telephone: 01732 865224.

Melbourne Hall, Melbourne, Deryshire DE73 1EN. Telephone: 01332 862502.

Osborne House, East Cowes, Isle of Wight PO32 6JY. Telephone: 01983 200022.

Powis Castle, Welshpool, Powys SY21 8RF. Telephone: 01938 554336.

Renishaw Hall, Renishaw, Derbyshire S31 9WB. Telephone: 01246 432042.

Rousham House, Steeple Aston, Oxfordshire. Telephone: 01869 347110.

Stourhead, Stourton, Mere, Wiltshire BA12 6QD (NT). Telephone: 01747 841152.

Stowe, Buckingham, Buckinghamshire MK18 5EH (NT). Telephone: 01280 822850.

Studley Royal, Ripon, North Yorkshire HG4 3DY (NT). Telephone: 01765 601002.

Waddesdon Manor, Waddesdon, Aylesbury, Buckinghamshire HP18 0JH (NT). Telephone: 01296 651211.

Wallington House, Cambo, Northumberland NE61 4AR (NT). Telephone: 01670 774283.

Wilton House, Wilton, Salisbury, Wiltshire SP2 0BJ. Telephone: 01722 743115.

Wrest Park, Silsoe, Bedford MK45 4HS. Telephone: 01525 860125 or 860178.

Index